Holding In,

Holding On

ARTIST'S BOOKS BY

Martha A. Hall

MORTIMER RARE BOOK ROOM

SMITH COLLEGE 2003

This catalogue accompanies a travelling exhibition of the artist's books of Martha Hall held at

The Mortimer Rare Book Room, Neilson Library, Smith College
(September–October 2003)

Special Collections, Margaret Clapp Library, Wellesley College
(November–December 2003)

The George J. Mitchell Department of Special Collections and Archives, Hawthorne-Longfellow Library, Bowdoin College
(January–March 2004)

The Arts of the Book Collection, Sterling Library, Yale University
(August–October 2004)

ISBN: 0-87391-053-2

Table of Contents

Martha Hall's Books

LETHA E. MILLS, M.D.

The art in Martha Hall's books will deeply affect each of us. The first impression may be of creativity, uniqueness, and beauty, but the second is the recognition of how a book can touch one's soul. Words alone often seem inadequate to express the depth of emotion we feel, or to convey the breadth of meaning we are capable of sensing. The visual language and lyric words of Martha's books will impact each of us differently, depending on our prior life experiences. For some, like me, there will be a message that stirs and translates to physical sensations. I have more than once completed reading a book with shivers coursing through me. It is a visceral response, a sense of being "hit in the gut," so great is the sense of identification. For a few, the power of the images or words will invoke difficult emotions or memories, and they will turn away. For many, especially those living with breast cancer or other serious disease, the books will be a source of comfort and understanding. Their viewing of Martha's work may recall shared experiences and help them move forward on their road to healing.

Before going further I think a common language will be helpful. What is healing? Although curing an illness may be one form of healing, it is not what I refer to here. Being on a path toward healing is to be striving toward a sense of wholeness or fulfillment of personal meaning. To be "healed" means to have achieved a feeling of psychological and spiritual well-being even though an illness may still be present.

Ideally, this striving for a sense of meaning forms the basis for how one learns to live. Whether meaning is pursuing our goals or appreciating the presence of loved ones in our lives, meaning is unique to the person and the time in one's life. Viktor Frankl, a survivor of the Nazi concentration camps, wrote in *Man's Search for Meaning,* "We can discover meaning in life in three different ways: (1) by creating a work or doing a deed; (2) by experiencing something or encountering someone (meaning can be found not only in work but also in love); and (3) by the attitude we take toward unavoidable suffering." He explains the third statement: "Even the victim of a hopeless situation, facing a fate he cannot change, may rise above himself, may grow beyond himself, and by doing so change himself." Martha's work and indeed her life are full of meaning.

I've known Martha Hall since 1993. A former professional weaver, she graduated from the Tuck School of Business at Dartmouth and, in fact, had initially been diagnosed with breast cancer just prior to her graduation. She received her adjuvant chemotherapy for the first six months of her new executive career in New York City by commuting to her home in Maine, receiving treatment on a Monday, returning on Tuesday. She was admonished by her supervisor to tell no one at work what she was undergoing on these long weekends away. She took these days as unpaid days, missing not only the emotional support but also the paid leave time bestowed on colleagues who had family members diagnosed with cancer. She came to me four years later as a patient with newly diagnosed recurrent breast cancer. She underwent rigorous chemotherapy followed by a stem cell transplant at Dartmouth, where I was practicing as a medical hematologist/oncologist. As she recovered from this therapy, she attended a workshop on "Cancer and Creativity," exploring creativity through writing, sculpture and dance. She moved on to a paste paper workshop where she began to make her books. Her first book, "The Raven," was completed in November 1996. She has made books for her daughters, Danielle and Gabrielle, and also for her husband, Alan. Other books eloquently describe her experiences with her disease and her interactions with the health care system. Over these last 6 years I have seen her move from being tentative in her exploration of her book-making into someone who lives life fully while continuing to grow artistically as she daily contends with metastatic breast cancer and the myriad side effects of its treatment.

For Martha (and others with metastatic cancer), additional symptoms may be treatment-related or they may herald progressive metastatic disease now at a new site. The same "old" chemotherapy drugs might today cause new symptoms. Toxicities may accumulate, and so increase with time. Drugs that were previously tolerated may cross-react with added medications and new toxicities may arise. This means each day may bring fresh concerns or may be a "good" day. How has she learned to live with an illness that is incurable today, but may be curable tomorrow? Her books help us to see. She has learned to have hope, and to make each moment count. This ability to live in the present and enjoy each day is something we all need to learn from her.

There are two levels of perception of illness. One we speak of easily, particularly in our culture of science as the basis for medicine, and that is the explanation of what is happening to our bodies on a physical, clinical level. That is what the computerized tomography (CT) scan reveals and the pathology report describes and names as a specific disease entity ("Infiltrating ductal carcinoma of the breast, stage II"). But the other is the very private, personal, and often unspoken perception. It may include fear, anxiety, guilt, sadness, blame, anger, or even misunderstanding. Too often people will deny these emotions or hide them in their struggle to cope. Certainly, psychotherapy offers one avenue of help, but art can also express life experiences. Deep feelings can be communicated more richly, without the need to label them, through art. Art can express painful, even conflicting emotions and by doing so be a catharsis. Also like psychotherapy, it is not judgmental.

Martha's stories will speak to each of us differently and their meaning will change as we change and grow. Her small book "Legacy" uses a skeleton dancing to tell the story that she and I spoke of years ago. She was struggling with how best to parcel out her finite physical energy. She was still working as an executive, but increasingly finding that her joy was in book making. At the same time, she was dealing with the fear of a possible premature death due to this breast cancer. I told her to consider her books as her legacy, so that whether she died sooner than she would have liked or lived many years, her books would always be a source of comfort, reflection and reminiscence.

She and I struggle to deal with the

health care system from different perspectives. As an oncologist, I continue to learn from her experiences and one of my hopes is that her books will affect many other physicians in the same way that they have heightened my self-awareness. May they cause physicians enough angst to seek and learn better communication skills and to realize that empathy and caring benefit both parties in a physician-patient relationship! Some of Martha's starkly negative moments in the health care system make it clear what emotional pain physicians sometimes carelessly inflict on patients with their thoughtless comments, superficial interactions, and uncaring behavior. We are taught to be masters of technology but explore little about our emotional selves. Her book "Small Rooms" depicts one of her experiences of dealing with uncomprehending health care providers. Its message exists on multiple levels. The structure and surface of the constructed book encompass the first sensation, the words and their story the second, and last is the impact of the emotional experience.

The medical evaluation of disease has become highly technical—CT scans, MRIs, bone scans, biopsies, blood tests—all take time to schedule, then to perform, and still more to have results determined, compared to previous studies, and our assessment communicated to the patient. This waiting can seem unbearable to a patient whose future hangs in the balance, determined by "how well they did" on the test. Martha's book "Test Day" is an example of what it is like to be the patient. She tells us she wants to know the details of her disease, but always in the context of hope. In other books she uses clear visual images of x-rays, bone scans, and photocopied pictures of prescription bottles and they communicate her powerful perceptions. Physicians need to see, feel, perceive, and care about what their patients are experiencing and then to advocate for a better system.

Too often though, costs of care are defining the type and duration of treatment. In addition, training in Western medicine teaches physicians to distance their feelings from their interactions with patients to protect themselves, but it may instead lead to emotional blunting and a less than empathetic approach. Being a patient makes us vulnerable. We need to be heard, understood, and cared for as unique persons, not as cases or as individuals defined only by our particular disease.

I believe a further role for these books in enhancing health care delivery is to empower patients and their health care providers to demand better care. Health care providers today are frequently as dissatisfied as their patients with the current system. If a culture of caring can be seen as necessary and of value, then members of the community can speak up and let doctors know what is needed. Doctors must work with others in the system to facilitate change. Martha's work can help make this happen. She inspires. I not only admire her remarkable talent and creativity, I love her for all that she is.

NOVEMBER 2003

Artist's Statement

The day before Mother's Day 1989, less than a month before I was due to receive my Master's in Business Administration from the Tuck School at Dartmouth, a surgeon I did not know phoned me. "You have breast cancer and you better decide quickly whether you're going to do something about it here [Dartmouth Hitchcock Hospital in Hanover, N.H.] or in Portland [Maine, the nearest major hospital to my home]. With that threat, he hung up.

I instinctively knew in those first moments of shock and tears that my life had just changed. I did not know then. that the diagnosis would alter my life in positive ways.

I was thirty-nine years old, married for eighteen years, with daughters in fifth and sixth grades. I was about to embark on a new career as a marketing executive at American Express. I was a former English teacher, weaver, sweater designer, and owner of a successful yarn retail and mail order business.

I underwent surgery, celebrated my fortieth birthday, graduated with honors from Tuck, had a second surgery, began six months of chemotherapy and a weekly commute to NYC for my job. I attended lectures and workshops for women with breast cancer; yet I told no one at work I was undergoing treatment. I worked long hours and earned promotions. I loved the high level of energy and intellect my job required and I made the most of living in New York. My odds of a full recovery were excellent; yet fear lurked within all my plans and dreams, especially those having to do with my family. I did not talk about the fear.

In spite of the fear and severe shoulder pain, I was shocked in 1993 when a routine test revealed I now had metastatic breast cancer. I underwent high dose chemotherapy treatment in Maine, then an autologous bone marrow transplant in Hanover, followed by radiation. I was exhausted, physically and emotionally, and spent months recovering. I sat and watched the birds outside my window.

The positive impacts of cancer on my life gradually became apparent. I left my job in New York City and began working in Maine; I joined a local support group; I spent much more time with my family. I participated in several writing and art workshops, and rediscovered my creativity through the making of artist's books.

I completed my first artist's book, "The Raven" in 1996. Its text, a poem about the fear of a second recurrence, came to me spontaneously; and, as with nearly all my subsequent books, it uncovered or *brought to light* emotions I had not previously acknowledged. In many of the early books I protected myself, albeit unconsciously, by using metaphors of journeys, seasons or gardens to illuminate my feelings about having cancer. I used established poets' work, rather than my own. I was holding back.

I shared these early books only with my family for two reasons. First, the books were very personal, emotional and revealing. Second, I did not have confidence in my artistic abilities. I tried various media, including photography and collage, to illustrate the texts, with mixed success. I discarded ideas when I could not think of a way to depict them graphically without having to draw or paint.

The artist's book "Tattoo," created in 1998, highlights breakthroughs for each of these concerns. The text tells eight short stories about my changing attitude toward people with tattoos. One of the stories is about a brash, tall, gay black man with a shaved head who shared a studio table with me in a book arts workshop. He frightened me until I saw that his tattoo was of Curious George. The story of George appears at the physical turning point of the book. When George saw a book I had made, he softly told me, "My mother died of breast cancer when I was sixteen. I wish I had thought to make art about it then." George's revelation helped me realize that it was important to stop holding in my feelings; and instead to share my work with others, including people I might never meet. I decided I would like my work to be in public collections, particularly college libraries.

The first college I approached was Wellesley College. Ruth Rogers, The Special Collections librarian of the Margaret Clapp Library decided to acquire a copy of "Tattoo" and also encouraged me to make the book in a small edition. Upon hearing this, my daughter, then a student at

Wellesley, put her arm around me and said, "Mom, you're a real artist now." When other college librarians and curators added "Tattoo" to their collections, I started to believe she was right. The year was 2000; I had been creating books since the fall of 1996.

As my book making skills increased I found catharsis in the physical act of making (and unmaking) books. When I pulled apart and reassembled a publication of the National Cancer Institute to create "What You Don't Want to Know about Cancer," the process of stitching, crumpling, tearing, cutting, and stapling the pages helped me express and release anger. "Voices: Five Doctors Speak" created in 1999 after my second recurrence, allowed me both to express anger and to have a positive impact on the way physicians interact with patients. When I showed it to each of the five doctors who were treating me, the book elicited responses of denial, disbelief, discomfort—and an empirical need to understand how the images were made and the book assembled. It also helped me to communicate and build better relationships with my physicians.

Anger runs through many of the books I create. It is there in terse sentences, irony, humor, color, images that cannot be understood, and in the mysterious language of medicine. I am not angry that I have breast cancer. I am angry that my mother was diagnosed with breast cancer a month after I was. I am angry that my daughters live under a cloud of fear about their own futures. I am angry that my husband has had to change his lifestyle; I am angry when people I know are diagnosed with cancer—or worse, *mis*diagnosed. I am angry that I have so much responsibility for telling the doctors when something is wrong. I am angry when women I know die; and I sob even when women I don't know die of breast cancer. I am angry that my doctors, in trying to protect me, endangered me. I am angry that there are no answers. But in some profound way, naming the emotions of anger, frustration, sorrow and fear; capturing with words and images those feelings on a page, helps to dissipate them.

Some of the pages in "Voices: Five Doctors Speak" also reflect my fear, which was validated in a direct but gentle way by my oncologist Letha Mills, who said, "In order to live you must live with the fear of dying." She also asserted that the books I was creating were more than a form of art therapy and that the books in themselves had an intrinsic value that would outlast me and become my legacy.

The process of making the books has been a powerful part of my healing. Some of the books have a life of their own it seems; pushing me to communicate a strong message. People may not want to "touch" the topics I explore in my books; yet the books invite handling, touching, interaction. They compel not only physical involvement with the book, but also involvement with the ideas expressed in the art and text. They help me to delve into feelings I did not know I had until I listened to what the books told me. They are a way to share my emotions with my family. They are a way to educate others about cancer. They are a way to touch the hearts of people who themselves are battling cancer or a life-threatening disease. They are a means to effect change in the way medical professionals interact with their patients. They are a way I can have a voice in the world. They are about making choices. They are about living.

The themes are universal and speak to family, friends and strangers: living with the fear of dying in order to live; creating to heal myself and others; leaving a legacy; appreciating and living fully each day.

I am an artist living with cancer. As the cumulative effect of being treated with weekly chemotherapy has made my hands clumsy, I have turned to others, notably a letterpress printer and a traditional bookbinder, to bring my ideas to fruition. It is difficult to seek and receive help, but the quality of their work and the developing professional relationships are invaluable. I am no longer a business executive.

My life with my husband is slower now, quiet, peaceful, happy. We are living our dreams on an island with a view of the ocean from every window in our home. I am more confident of my poetry and art, and I find joy in writing, printing images, and painting large sheets of paper. I enjoy the challenge of finding or devising book structures that give wings to the words and images I have created. I am honored that my books are of interest to others. They have helped me heal, helped me to live fully. They will be my legacy.

APRIL 2003

It's all right to cry.

—MARGARET ROLAND, M.D.

MARCH 1997

Just to Live

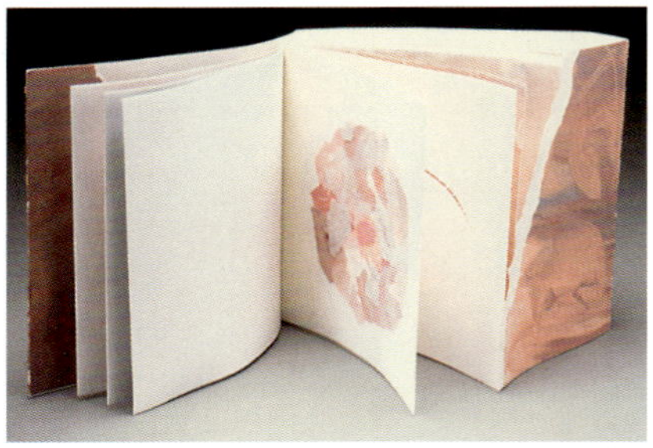

MARCH 1997

Just to Know

Excerpt

I will have this test today and then I will know. Know what? Know that I have cancer? Possibly. Not probably. Possibly, I tell myself. The word calms me. It seems small. But I will never again know that I *don't* have cancer. And that is so hard. So hard to carry in my heart. So hard to carry in my head. So impossible to explain.

And that not knowing touches everything I do, everything I decide, everything I struggle to plan. Everything.

"Take in a deep breath. Hold it." The test. The technician's voice sounds eerie, comes from a speaker in the machine. She is in the other room, eyes on the computer, not me. The machine whirs softly as if something is spinning around and around at high speed inside. "Breathe." The machine moves forward a fraction of an inch. "Take in a deep breath. Hold it." Then the muted whirling sound. "Breathe." Again and again. Perhaps a hundred times. She must be tired of repeating the same phrase.

I look at the little light; listen for the rhythm of her voice then the machine; try not to think. I move my fingers slowly, imperceptibly to touch the rock in my pocket. Lucky rock, black with white stripe. I put it in my pocket this morning. I put Danielle's gift of the brown salmon-painted smooth stone in the other pocket. Wore my bright pink socks with the fish. A hug from Alan for luck.

Luck. Luck of the odds. Today's luck has been determined long before this day. So why do I carry its reminders? Pagan prayers? I do not feel it was bad luck that this happened. That I've had cancer. It just happened. No commentary. Some days I think it's genes.

Hope it is, because then it is not my fault; not something I have done or not done. Hope it is not, because then it is preordained; then nothing I do can change things. Painful irony. Complex confusion.

I want the test results to be good — or not bad, given the uncertainty of good results. For days I've traveled different paths in my mind. Convinced myself over and over that I'm okay. That I have no steady pain. No dark hints. And then I chastise myself. It's not safe to be too sure. What will you do if it's not good news? What then? I need to prepare myself. Take nothing for granted. But then, why worry about the bad unless it happens? Around and around the thoughts go, for days, nights. I am tired, tense for weeks before the test; even worse until I hear the results.

I play scenarios out in my mind. What treatments are there for me? Are there treatments for me? How sick will I be? How much time do I have? How much time can I gain? At what price? At what cost in time? What about the girls away in school? Work? What do I want to do with my time? And if I would think of doing something different with that time than I am doing now, then why am I doing what I'm doing now?

And then it's as if time starts again. Good news or bad news, the results set my life clock back to zero. And because it matters so much, I take luck into these hospital rooms. I take prayer into these rooms. I take all my strength, force of will. And I take my fear. I want those prayers and that luck to make a difference. I'm not sure I believe they do.

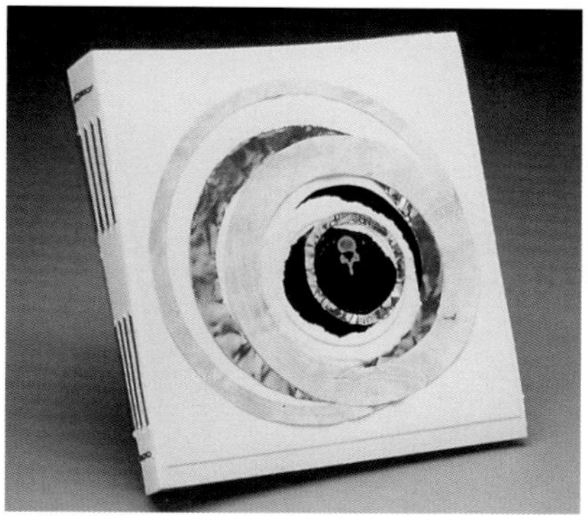

Other doctors should see this. Other cancer patients should see this.

—RODGER PRYZANT, M.D.

JULY 1998

Living

I hate the term cancer survivor.
It implies some people win
Some people lose.
It implies there is a point in time
When there is an answer.
I am living with cancer.
The emphasis is on living.

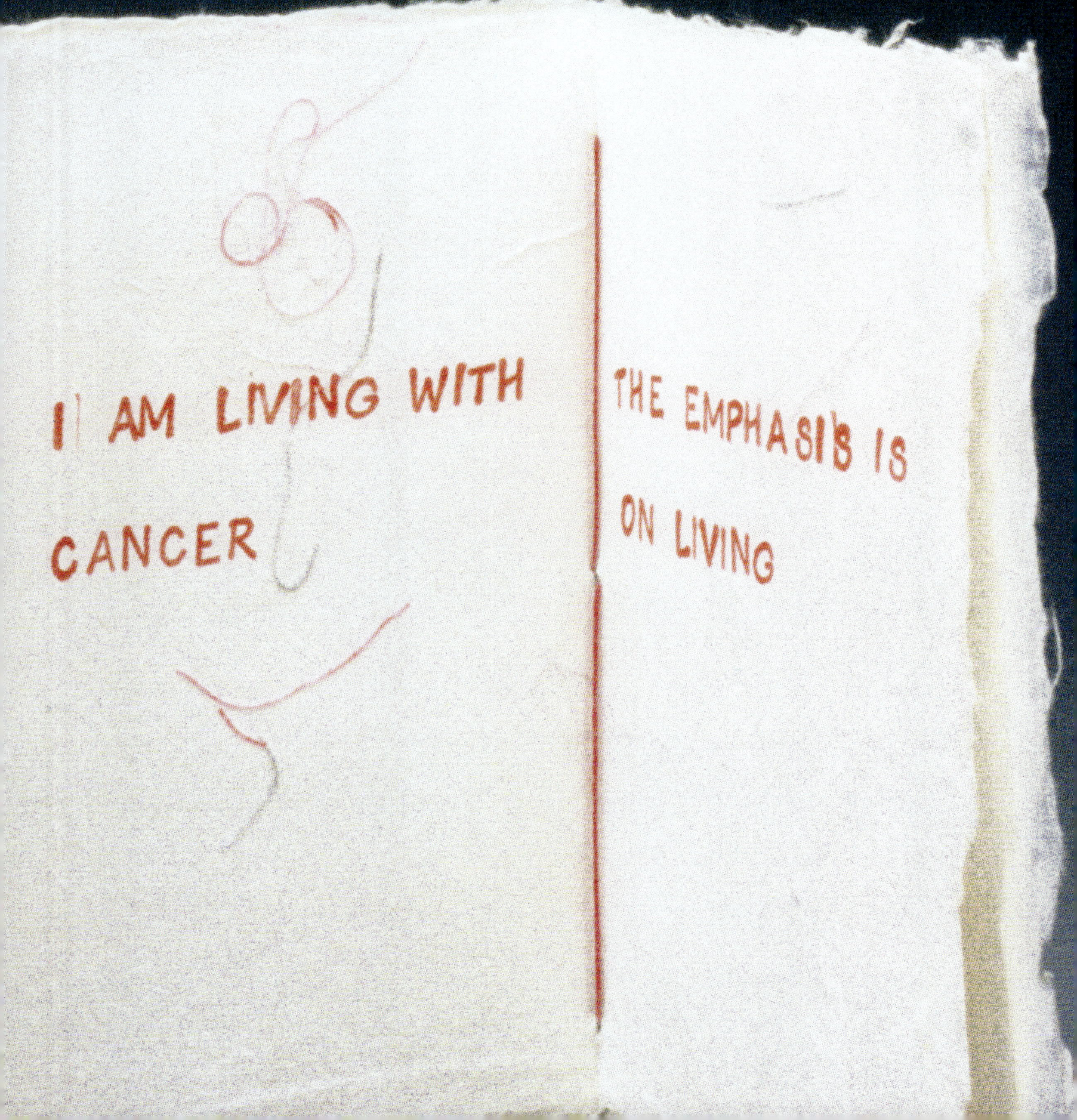
I AM LIVING WITH
CANCER
THE EMPHASIS IS
ON LIVING

AUGUST 1998

Voices: Five Doctors Speak

H: These are angry cells. They could
 be A or B or C.
 Let's find a quiet place to talk.
 The pathology shows breast cancer.

E: Let's take this one step at a time.
 I'm sorry.
 Do you want to speak to me on
 the phone or in person?
 There are many treatment
 options,
 There are two major players we
 haven't used yet.
 Taxol. Herceptin. Taxol.
 Herceptin. Taxol. Herceptin.
 We are buying time.

T: Your bone scan is fine.
 Your CT scan is fine.

M: Four and a half years is not bad.
 What's been going on in your life
 in the last few months?
 Your bone scan looks good.
 Your CT scan looks good.
 This is not about IF; this is
 about WHEN.
 It could be six months.
 It could be six years.
 In order to live, you must live
 with the fear of dying.

 Your books will be your legacy
 for family and for friends.
 And if you live to be an old lady
 You'll reminisce.

P: This will work.
 You are my poster child.
 You've done so well.

 We'll treat you with radiation
 two times a day for five days,
 then a week off.
 We'll do this four times,
 eight weeks in all.

You may experience a sore throat.
You may have difficulty swallowing.
You may be very tired.
I'll know if the radiation is
working.
I'll be able to feel it.

E: Two recurrences in nine years is
not bad.

It will be slow to go away.
It was slow to grow.

We won't know if Arimidex is
working.
We'll be working in the dark.

I felt it two months ago. I didn't
want to believe you'd failed.
The bone marrow transplant
failed.

You are responsive to chemo.

We failed.

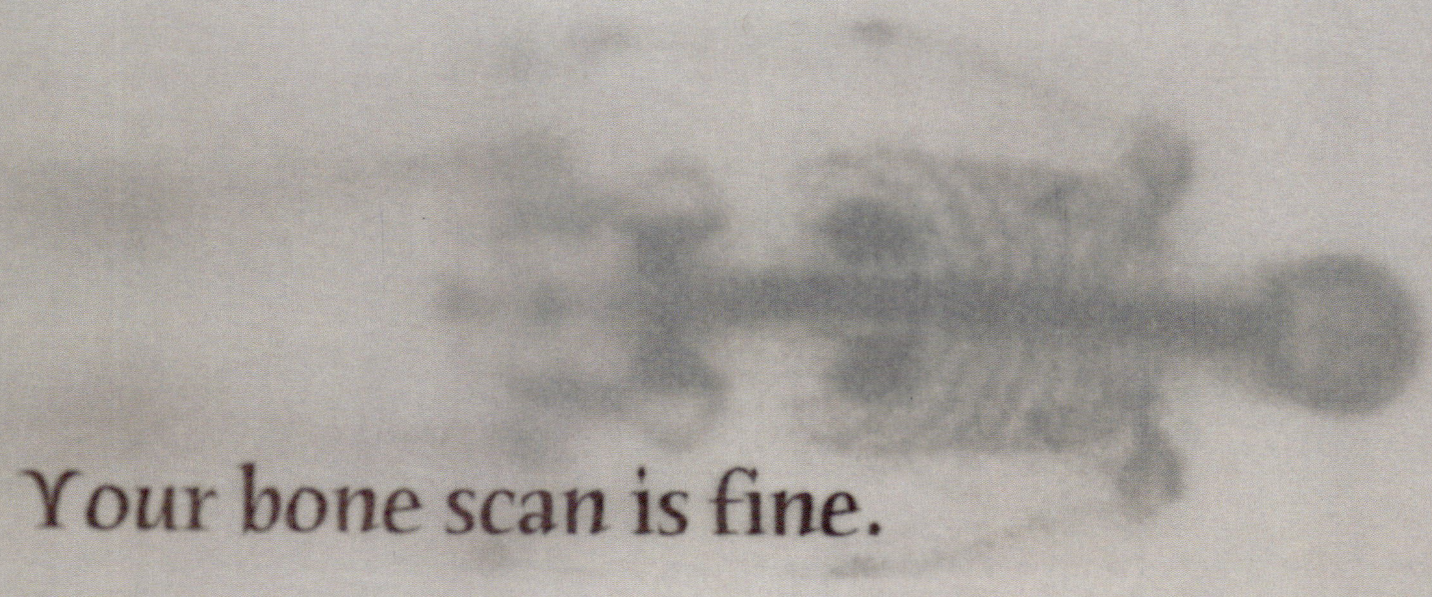

Your bone scan is fine.

Your CT scan is fine.

You failed.

What are you taking for pain?

What are your work plans?

I'm sorry. I'm sorry. I'm sorry.
I'm sorry. I'm sorry. I'm sorry.
I'm sorry. I'm sorry. I'm sorry.
I'm sorry. I'm sorry. I'm sorry.
I'm sorry. I'm sorry. I'm sorry.
I'm sorry. I'm sorry. I'm sorry.
I'm sorry. I'm sorry. I'm sorry.
I'm sorry. I'm sorry. I'm sorry.
I'm sorry. I'm sorry. I'm sorry.
I'm sorry. I'm sorry. I'm sorry.
I'm sorry. I'm sorry. I'm sorry.
I'm sorry. I'm sorry. I'm sorry.
I'm sorry. I'm sorry. I'm sorry.
I'm sorry. I'm sorry. I'm sorry.
I'm sorry. I'm sorry. I'm sorry.
I'm sorry. I'm sorry. I'm sorry.
I'm sorry. I'm sorry. I'm sorry.
I'm sorry. I'm sorry. I'm sorry.
I'm sorry. I'm sorry. I'm sorry.
I'm sorry. I'm sorry. I'm sorry.
I'm sorry. I'm sorry. I'm sorry.
I'm sorry. I'm sorry. I'm sorry.
I'm sorry. I'm sorry. I'm sorry.
I'm sorry. I'm sorry. I'm sorry.
I'm sorry.

VOICES:
Tom Ervin, M.D.
William Herbert, M.D.
Hector Tarraza, M.D.
Letha Mills, M.D.
Rodger Pryzant, M.D.

NOVEMBER 1998

Tattoo

I

When I was a child, I would steal
glances at my grandfather's tattooed
blue anchor —
only sometimes visible on his tanned
forearm, just below his khaki
sleeve.
I wasn't sure if I was supposed to see it.
I thought, "Tattoos must have some-
thing to do with the navy,
or going to sea, or that war that
happened long ago."
I had seen them only on white haired
men.

II

Years ago we took our small
daughters to the lake
and found it changed.
The crowd was rough, loud —
like the motorcycles they had arrived
on.
They were "not like us."
Even the women had tattoos.
We called the beach "Tattoo Beach"
and never went back.

III

A few years ago my daughter Danielle
gave me a postcard.
It is a black and white photo of a
nude woman with her arms out-
stretched.
She has a vine with flowers tattooed
on the scar across her missing breast.
I hung the card up on my studio door.
I admire the woman's courage,
her joy,
her beauty,
her defiance.

IV

This summer at Haystack I shared a
studio table with George from
Philadelphia,
a very tall black man with a shaved
head
who made complex, powerful,
angry art.
He was loud, brash, gay.
I was afraid of him —

Then I heard him sing in a beautiful
    soprano voice as he worked
and saw that the tattoo on his
    muscular brown arm was

Curious George.

One night he looked at the book I
    was making
called "Living"
and told me that when he was sixteen
his mother had died of breast cancer.

V
Last month I sat in art class next to a
    young woman who had blue rubber
    bands wrapped around her middle
    finger.
I was wrong.
They were not rubber bands,
but tattoos.
After class our instructor admired
    this young woman's tattoos
and bared her own self-inflicted art.

The young woman had pricked a blue
    ring on her finger;
The older woman a wide blue
    bracelet on her wrist.
The two women talked of the ink
    they'd used, the needles, the time
    it took,
the pain.
I couldn't believe any woman would
    do that to herself.

VI

Thursday night at an art show opening, I stood in the gallery with two other artists.
We talked about our tattoos —
blue dots to mark radiation's burn —
reminders that make us sad,
frightened,
angry,
grateful to be alive.
I have blue dots on my hip;
one now even on my chin.
There are three in a row above the scar on my blank left chest.
One of the women pulled down the neckline of her dress to show us a blue dot
centered between her breasts, now gone.
We compared our tattoos, standing there in the art gallery among the guests,
as if this were an ordinary thing to do.
then we laughed,
"Maybe we should connect the dots."

VII

Now I think I want a real tattoo —
a symbol used long ago
by courageous female warriors
It could be my symbol of the courage, power, and strength I need to fight my cancer.
It could be my prayer flag.

VIII

Will I dare to prick the surface?
Will it help to add another scar?

T

DECEMBER 1998

What You Don't Want to Know

DECEMBER 1998

Black Box

(contains 10 black and white books)

Excerpts

A few days after I was
first diagnosed
with breast cancer
I sat on the deck of our boat
reading a book
that a friend had given me
about a cancer survivor.

When I heard that day
on the radio
that she had died.
I threw the book into the sea.
I will never again read a book
about a "cancer survivor."

What I don't want to hear about:
hair loss
palliative treatment
metastases
lung damage
heart damage
radiation-increased risk of recurrence
slash and burn
survival rate
odds
life expectancy
life insurance refused
memory loss
chemo-induced menopause
infertility
CT, Bone Scan, MRI
low blood counts
vomiting
diarrhea
mouth sores
lymphedema
loss of fingernails
weight gain

HOPE
prevent the disease.
Tamoxifen (Nolvadex
Continued from Page 1C
Herceptin, the drug approved by the Food and Drug Administration in September, is based on the idea that a protein called HER-2/neu causes the unchecked growth of cancer cells. Another exciting area of research involves medications that address angiogenesis, which can cause tumors to develop new blood cells, allowing them to grow and spread.
"Cancer is a disease of growth," Wu says.
10 JUL 98
women with breast
year study to exam
could prevent the dis
women was halted
year early – after col
idence that the drug
of breast cancer by 4
the first study to sh
may be effective in
disease.
Though the FD
proved the use o
healthy women who
very high risk of d
cancer, controversy
role in prevention is
Experts hav

exhaustion
joints ache
lymph node involvement
recurrence
stage IV
increased risk for ovarian cancer
no safe estrogen replacement therapy
"We don't know."
increased risk for a second primary
breast cancer
my daughters' risk
chemotherapy
hospitalization
side effects
osteoporosis
intravenous feeding
blood transfusions
low counts
shingles
no cure

I should write, "What I don't want to hear about *again*."

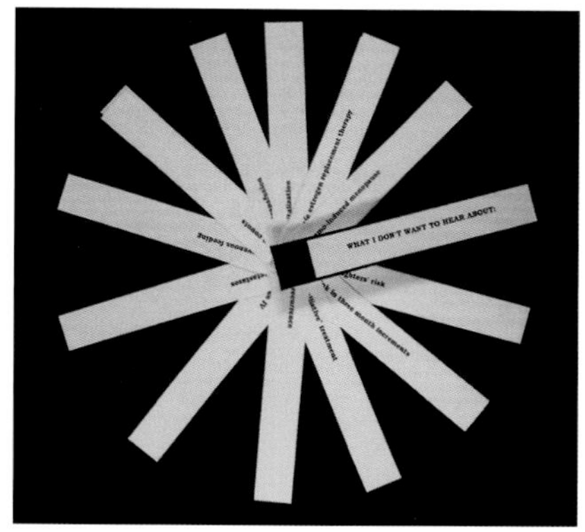

FEBRUARY 1999

Test Day

I hate it when the postcard comes.
I want to RSVP no,
As if it were an invitation
Not a command.

I will be obedient,
As if my desire to please
Will earn me good grades,
A passing mark.
Small child thoughts
In my woman head.

I will go
And take off my clothes,
Leave one breast in a locker,
Sit johnnie-waiting in cold halls.
I will hold my arms overhead
Sending floods of radiation
Through my bones,
Searing my lungs with eerie light.
I will do as I am told.

I will light up their screens,
My insides black and white.
Circles, shadows, lines.
But the watchers will not see me;
Will not see my self, my soul;
Will not see my fear.
My anger is hot, unspoken,
Black
It does not cloud
Their machine vision;
It does not melt their cold.

They are distant.
A glowing screen,
An apron heavy with lead,
A little room, door shut
Keep them safe from me.
Safe from knowing
That I fear what they may see.
Safe from listening.
Their only words,
"Take a deep breath"
"Hold it."
"You can breathe."

MARCH 1999

Sisters

Excerpts

Once I had 3
sisters, now there
is only one.
—GEE (*my mother*)

I told him
"If you
make me choose
I will always
pick my
sister."
—GABRIELLE *(my older daughter)*

Our names rhyme.
We even sound alike.
But I never wanted to acknowledge
any similarities with Gabrielle.
It's hard to be an individual;
even harder as a little sister.
But when we both went away to
school,
I started to realize how much I
admire
her strength and intelligence.
I guess I don't mind stating our
similarities any more,
when I wish I could be like her.
Sometimes.
—DANIELLE *(my younger daughter)*

I told him
"if you
make me choose
I will always
pick my
sister."
-gabriella

APRIL 1999

Dark Room Days

My days have been dark
dangerous.
I am drowning
in dread
dealing with death
despair
daughters' dilemmas
danger.
I miss the sun.

I have dark room days,
disturbed dreams.

Where are life's colors?

daughters'
dilemmas
TM

DECEMBER 1999

It's Nothing

Before we started to draw the skull in art class, we held our own skulls cupped in our hands. It was the first time I had come to class bald; the first time there was an exposed symbol of my cancer.

We gently moved out fingers down our vertebrae, felt for our first rib — collar bone — mine dense in a bed of unforgiving scar tissue. Old damage. Old healing.

The next week we traced our sternum, pushed on our ribs. I hated doing it. I hated knowing where the jabs of pain would be — long ago memorized.

Two people laughed at the edge of our group. I was too caught up in my own fears to hear why they were laughing.

My pain started in the night — or when I was driving. Surprising me; frightening me. I'd knead the area with my fingers, trying to find the exact spot of pain.

The pain was most often in a rib under my right breast. I thought about marking it with an X — saying, "There it is! There! — the place with the pain you can't explain."

I asked you, Dr. Ervin, guided your hand to the spot and said, "There! There I have pain over and over. Why?" Your answers were different each time — maybe arthritis, maybe old injuries, maybe you didn't want to tell me.

I told you, Dr. Mills, and showed you my un-marked X. And you said since the tests and scans showed nothing; since the counts were good, it *was* nothing. Nothing. You're fine. Don't worry.

I called you, Dr. Ervin, from the payphone at Haystack. The pain was so intense I could not breathe. But there were no pharmacies closer than Bangor which stocked stronger pain medicine than I already had. "It will get better in time."

When routine blood tests in September had "wrong" answers, you sent me for a bone scan which showed dark "hot spots" on my ribs. There. There where I had shown you I had pain. There. There where I had told you.

Only now there were many lines, pointing to my skull, my spine, both hips, my shoulders, rib after rib. My liver. You only told me about my hips — where it had been before — and my liver.

Your medical notes of 10-1-99, Dr. Ervin, read, "PT's in with progressive disease. She has multi-focal bony mets & multiple nodules in the liver. It appears she has new lesions consistent with the bone mets as well."

"Aches which she has minimized and really brought out fully today."

"Slightly more depressed than she has been in the past."

So in art class I draw my ribs, my vertebrae, my skull. I draw my pain. I draw delicacy that hides anger, fragility that holds strength. These are my bones. I need to draw them to heal.

I draw my bones on the days I have Taxol, Herceptin, Pamidronate. Drugs to heal my ribs, my skull, my spine, my hips.

I will keep listening — to hear what my bones are saying.

Think in three month increments.

—TOM ERVIN, M.D.

MARCH 2000

Inside Out

APRIL 2000

Blue Moon

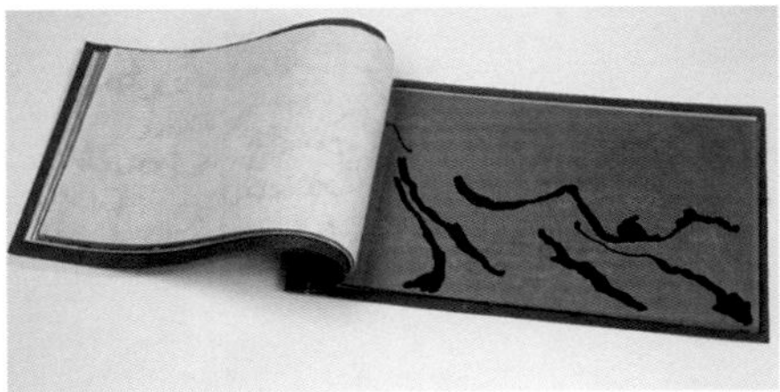

"Once in a blue moon," my mother
   used to say.
Last year there were two months with
   blue moons.
This year there are none.

My body is adorned with circles and
   lines —
a human landscape designed by
   surgeon's hands —
not God.

My breast, once round, is a cave in
   this new landscape.
The medical port, a raised mound
   under my scarred chest wall,
is not a substitute.

I am old before it is time.
Chemo has etched the early smile
   lines around my eyes
into deep ravines where no tears
   flow.

Emotions run too deep to reach even
   this once easy release.

I lie in my island bed,
my skin as dry as if I were an old
   woman—
dry even to my lover's touch.

Even the moon's pull is not enough
to give me back the lost river of blood.

The undertow of death pulls me down,
and I struggle to the surface.
Old, older —
but still I swim.

I cannot wait for the elusive blue moon.
I cannot wait for its strong pull
to bring back lost rhythms of life.

Instead, I watch the tides each day
Their coming and going,
an affirmation

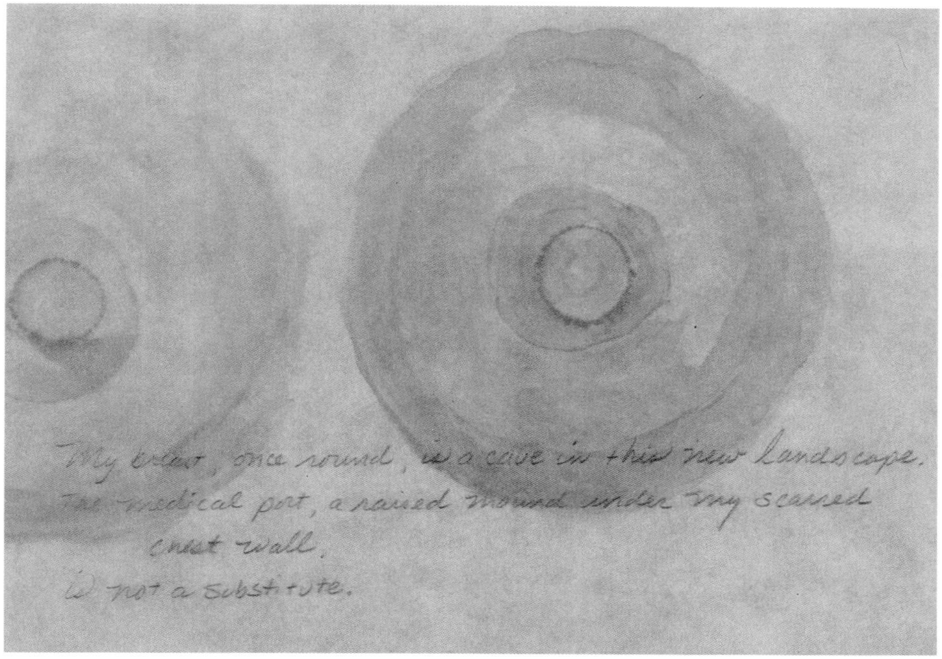
My breast, once round, is a cave in this new landscape.
The medical port, a raised mound under my scarred
chest wall,
is not a substitute.

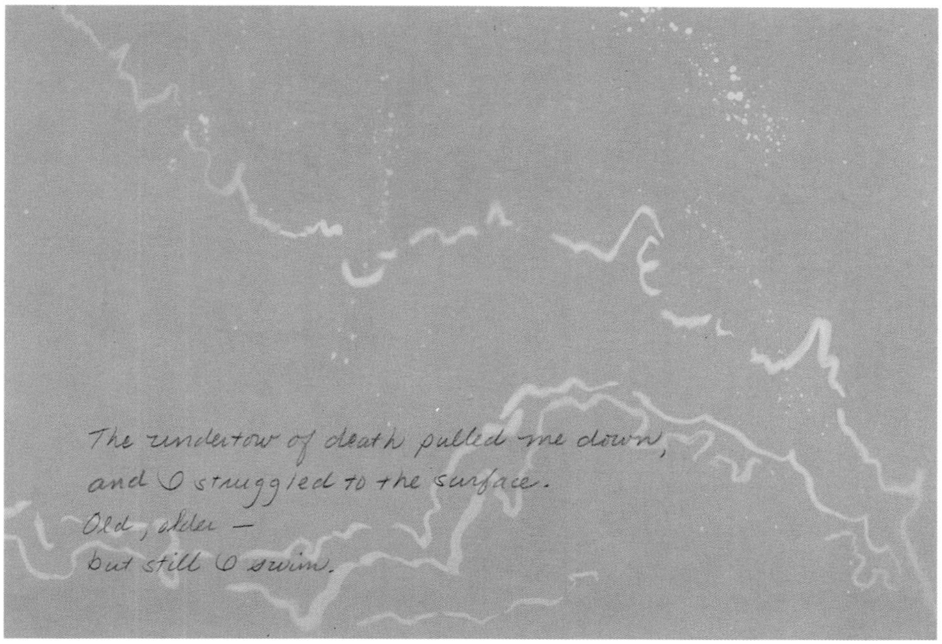
The undertow of death pulled me down,
and I struggled to the surface.
Old, older —
but still I swim.

JUNE 2000

One Week from Today

I must have an X-ray on Monday,
one week from today.

They will search for cancer
in the bone behind my eye.

Let there be another answer—
wintergreen, solvents,
printer's ink.

I have stood this week in the sun,
pulling color from the water
onto my pages.

I have heard the stories of the
  blacksmith with pearls,

and seen the grace and intensity of
  the juggler.

I have seen coiled ropes in the
wet woods—
wondered if made by artist or fisherman.

I have held a salted fish in my hands,
its scales pearlescent inspiration.

This week I am an artist.

Next week is one week from today.

NOVEMBER 2000

The Rest of My Life

It has been
more than a year
since I was diagnosed
with a recurrence
of breast cancer.
Friends ask, "How much longer?"
They mean, "When will chemo be
done?"
"When will you be back at work?"
Last week a woman
who sat next to me in the chemo
room said,
"I have only one more treatment to go.
When will you be through?"
Last time, and the time before,
and the time before that,
I could answer,
"I have two more treatments left."
"Next month"
or
"I'm halfway through."

Now,
what is the answer?
"Never."
"Until I die."
or
"As long as I live."
"Until there is a new treatment."
"Until this treatment stops working."

There is no answer.
I don't have an answer.
The doctors don't have an answer.

YES — But I have ways to answer:
"I am living with cancer."
"I am buying time."
"I have a chronic disease."
I'll be back for more treatment
on Monday."

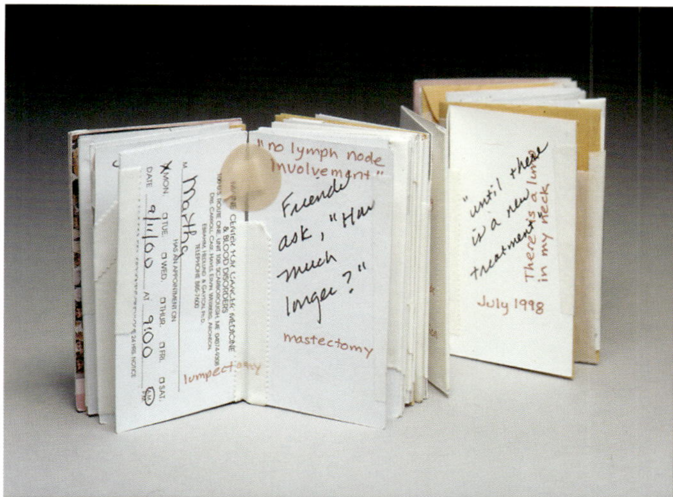
"no lymph node involvement"
Friends ask, "How much longer?"
mastectomy
"until there is a new treatment"
July 1998

MAINE CENTER FOR
Cancer Medicine
Blood Disorders

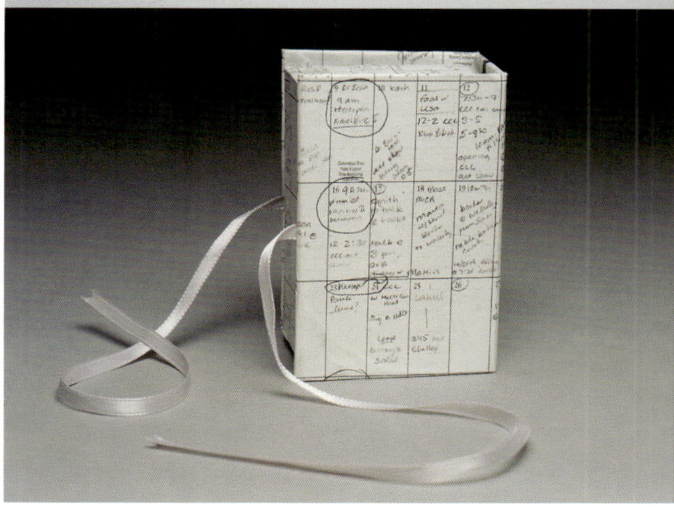

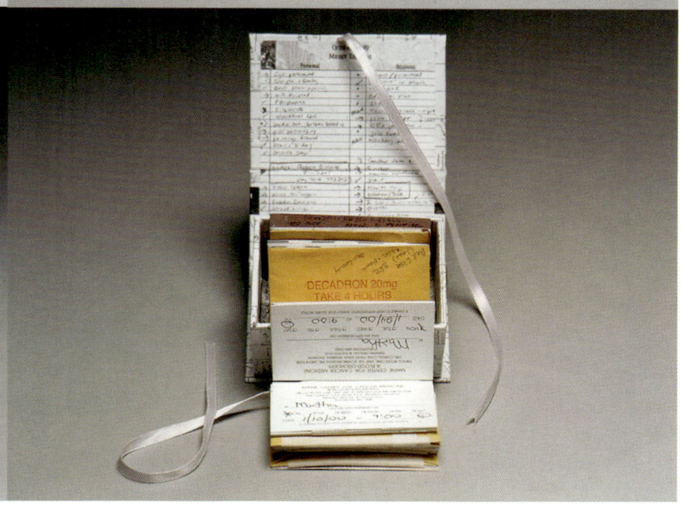
DECADRON 20mg
TAKE 4 HOURS

Jane, with Wings

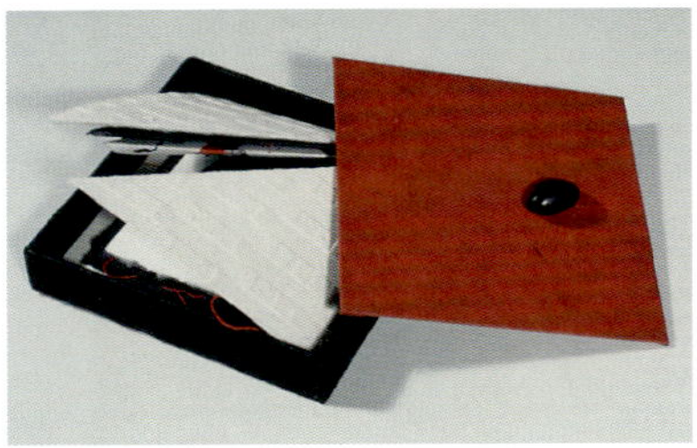

There is a pattern
in the darkness —
a crack
in the middle,
or on the edge,
on the out
or on the in —
stitched together
and coming apart.

Do you see
what
you
fear?

Close it away.
The fear . . .
Close this page.

You are not
the one
who is dying.

You do not
need to see
beneath the surface
the skin,
the scars.

You are not
the one
the skin,
the scars.

MAY 2001

Anxiety (to Martin Antonetti)

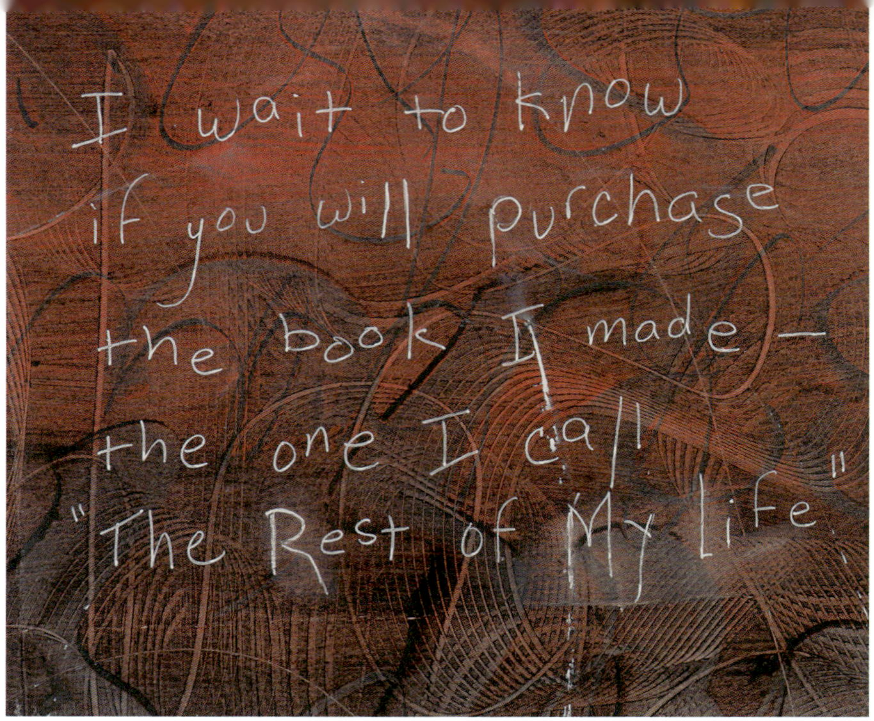

I have been waiting
nearly three weeks
for you to call —
or is it three days . . .

I want to know
If you will purchase
the book I made —
the one I call
"The Rest of My life."

Yesterday your answer
was all important to me.

Today I do not care.

Last night I felt
— then saw —
the rocky lump
on my sternum.

This morning I called
my doctor, then drove
like a wild woman to see him
— one hour away —
Knowing he had postponed
his leaving to examine me.

I held my arms high
while he pushed
against my skin —
here — here, here —
Then he gave me a hug
and sent for an X-ray.

Tonight he will call me
about
The Rest of My Life.

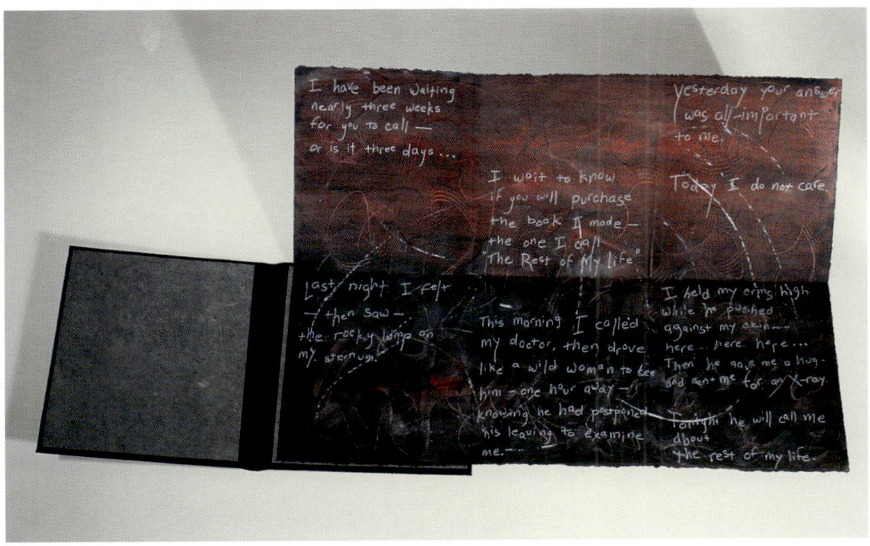

JULY 1997

What Will Be My Legacy?

How much time
will I have?

What will make
a difference?

What will be my
legacy?

MARCH 2001

Legacy

Your books
will be your legacy,
for family
and for friends.
And if you live
to be an old lady
you'll reminisce.

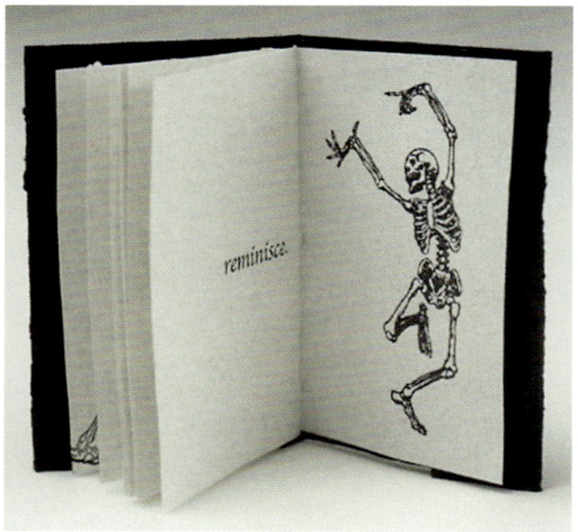

MAY 2001

I Make Books

I make books.
I write what I cannot say.
I make marks with meaning only in
  their making.
I paint in colors fearsome and strange.
I make books so I won't die.

AUGUST 2001

Ghost Friends

I cry when I read
Your obituary,
Remember your face,
Your daughters
And our conversations.

I cry that there is no cure.
I cry in relief
That this time
It is not me,
I cry in surging sadness
That it is you.

ROBERTA

Roberta found treasures for Alan and me: a wooden knitting stick carved with "Martha Hall 1845" and a large photograph of the historic Yarmouth shipyards. She bought a spinning wheel from us the week before she died.

VI

When our redhead daughters were babies, Vi and I had tea and talk. Twenty years later, when Vi too had a recurrence of breast cancer, she did not return my calls.

HEATHER

I always cry when I see the words of Heather's daughter, etched in the glass of Heather's collage:

"What are your breasts filled with now, Mommy?" said eight-year-old Elisabeth.

"Saline, like salt water," I said.

"Oh," said Elisabeth, after a moment, "you mean like tears."

"Yes, my darling, my breasts are filled with tears."

PENNY
At Heather's funeral, Penny mused, "I wonder which of us will be next?" Her words were such a sad irony.

ADA
Ada took all the money from her retirement account, paid the penalties, and left to visit her sisters. She died in the Midwest, her heart ravaged by chemo.

CATHY
A stranger wheeled a tiny skeleton of a woman into our "Creativity and Women with Cancer" workshop, told us the sleeping woman's name was Cathy, then left. Cathy raised her head only once, to ask for more morphine.

JAMIEN
One summer I made paper with bits of tea in it for a book I planned to call "Transformation." I wanted to honor Jamien who sent invitations each year to women around the world, inviting them to have tea with friends at 4 p.m. on the first day of spring.

I never made the book. Jamien's life was too large for my pages.

JEAN
Jean always smelled like bananas. She'd been to Mexico to find a cure.

Jean's daughter was shaking when she told me her mother no longer recognized her.

JULIE
PENNY

JO

My best friend Holly's mom let her have comic books and soda. She gave the best birthday parties ever — especially the pirate party!

When my mother took me to see Mrs. Phillips in the hospital, I thought this must be someone else my mother knew.

MARY

When Mary, a physician and blue water sailor, told our support group she could not come anymore, we turned our heads away. I am still ashamed.

JULIE

She could make everyone laugh in our support group, "I was fine before I met you guys; but then I came to one of your meetings and caught cancer from you all!"

She was the Valentine Bandit, decorating Portland with hundreds of hearts tacked on telephone poles. The Portland papers made much of the mystery, and Julie became an unknown celebrity. When she had her bone marrow transplant, her friends decorated the hospital corridors with hearts

NANCY

I was at a conference where a stately, beautiful bald woman stood asking questions of the doctors. I did not want to know the answers. I was glad she asked the questions.

SANDY

It was as if Sandy believed that a positive attitude would save her. She slipped into denial, not wanting cards, calls, support group, visitors.

She cooked a turkey for our family when I was ill.

JOYCE

Joyce walked into the treatment room and told us, the regulars, she had decided not to have chemo, not to fight anymore. She would not be coming back. Her husband was crying.

ELLEN

The next time Ellen came into my yarn shop she told me about traveling by train to California to surprise her daughter — ringing the doorbell, then hiding in the bushes, jumping out when the door opened. She spoke to me in a whisper, wheeling her oxygen tank. She bought yarn to knit a baby sweater for her new granddaughter.

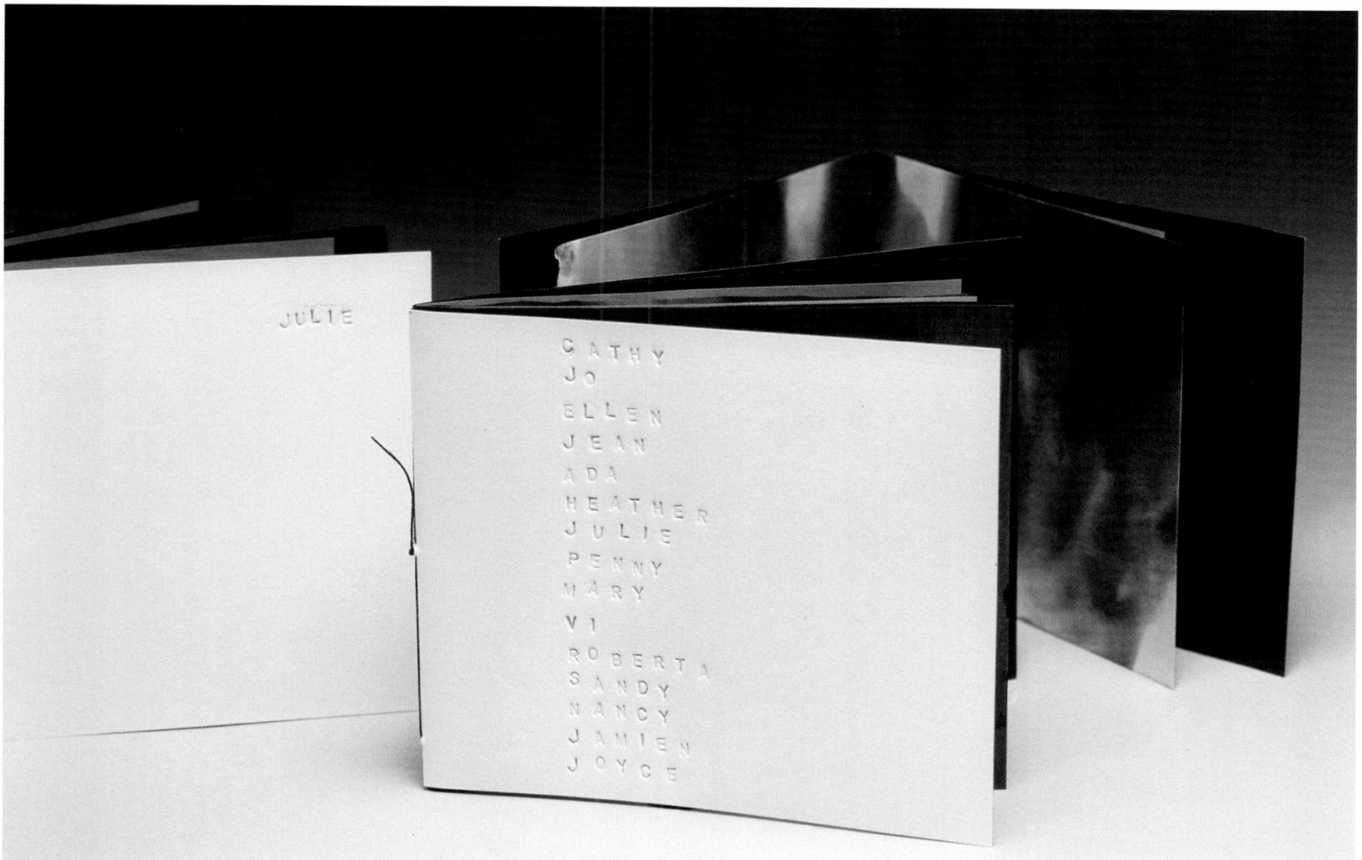
JULIE
CATHY
JO
ELLEN
JEAN
ADA
HEATHER
JULIE
PENNY
MARY
VI
ROBERTA
SANDY
NANCY
JAMIEN
JOYCE

Do not worry.
There is nothing to be
concerned about.

—SKIP WILKIS, M.D.

MARCH 2002

Small Rooms

The building is new.

The corridor is long,
too long.

Women with offices stand outside
their doors gossiping.

There is only one bathroom.
A line of women waits.

There is no changing room.

There is no place to put my clothes.
I fold them, bra inside
and put them on the basket
where the used gowns go.

You can see the parking lot
and Route One
from the examining room.

Why do I have to take off my socks?

The nurse asks, "And how are you
today?"

I answer, "I'm in terrible pain."

and she responds, "Oh.
I like the color of your sweater."

She doesn't look at me.

Then she tells me I am wrong.
I can't still be on chemo.
People take chemo for only six months.

Why did I have to fill out pages
if neither the doctor or nurse looks at
them?

I don't want to recite the saga.

She is wearing a pink ribbon pin.
She stands up and ushers me
to a small room.

24Jan2002

Now it is the doctor's turn to ask,
"And how are you today?"

He does not give me time
to answer.
He talks about politics
as he examines me.

"What is Xeloda?" he asks.
"What about Pamidronate?"
"Is Taxotere the same as Taxol?"
"Is Herceptin new?"

These are the chemotherapies
that keep me alive.
He cannot even pronounce them.

Then he says, "You're fit as a fiddle!"

I think, "That's easy for you to say."
I hope my eyes will not spill their tears.

When he asks if I have any questions
I say, "None that you can answer."
I suppose I am being rude.
I hope so.

"See you next year."

No.
I am not coming here next year.
I will find another gynecologist.
before then.

I don't tell him that.
Perhaps I should.
Perhaps I should tell him why.

Instead I pay the bill and leave.

I leave the long corridors,
the waiting women,
the nurses and doctors asking
someone else,
"And how are you today?"

I'm "fit as a fiddle."
I have stage IV breast cancer.

APRIL 2002

Test Results, January 2002

When my doctor showed me the bone scan
and said that the lesions on my ribs were the same as last time
and the tumor in my liver was no longer visible,
I was happy . . .

but
I still cannot let go of the fear.

APRIL 2002

Prescriptions

When my stomach is on fire,
I do not know which prescription to
take.
None of them seems to work.

Ativan helps with pain.

Ativan makes me fell mellow, gentle,
floaty.
The nurses wouldn't give it to me
yesterday
because I had no one to drive me home.
I worry that I will become addicted.

I hate being incoherent — unable to
finish sentences.

My high energy days I wonder if it is
me or the drugs.

When I first started taking Tylox,
I lived alone in an apartment in
New York City.
I had to take so many for the pain
that I worried I wouldn't wake up
and no one would find me.

If I took pills for pain while I was at
work,
I wondered how I sounded, and how
I acted.
Was I still me?

Some nights when I cannot sleep,
I take a second sleeping pill.
I then sleep late and wake up with a
foggy brain.

I have three bottles of Lomotil which
helps with diarrhea —
one for the car, one for my purse,
the third for the bathroom.
I seldom have warning that I will
need it.

I usually have nausea for three days
after I have chemo.
I sometimes feel so bad that when
I go looking for the medicine,
I fumble with the jars.
Which one works most quickly?
Which one is least likely to send me
into space?

Some of the prescriptions tell me not
to drive
or not to have alcohol.
What about the others which don't
say that?
Will I just be okay?

I called the doctor to ask what order
I should take the prescriptions in.
How long did I need to wait to see if
the first pills worked?
And what if they don't?
What was the next prescription to
try?

How long did I need to wait to see if
this one worked?

Can I take these two prescriptions
together?
How am I supposed to know?

The pharmacist always asks do I have
any questions
and I always say no.

I take four Xeloda a day.
I used to take seven, but that was
too toxic.
Am I taking enough now to hold back
my cancer?

I have too many prescriptions.

Sometimes I get home from the phar-
macy with a new prescription —
and can't remember what it's for.

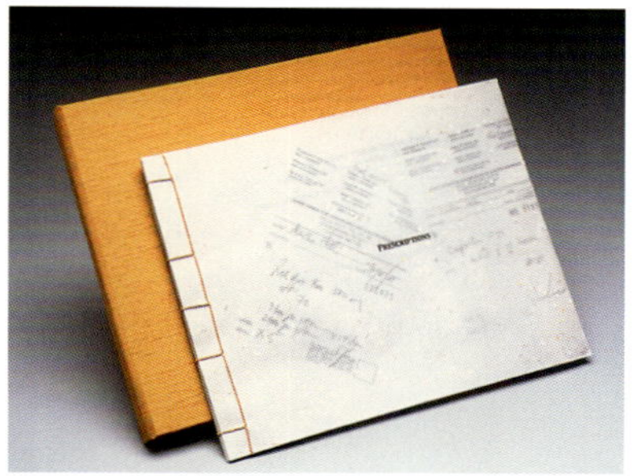

SOMETIMES I GET HOME FROM THE PHARMACY WITH A NEW PRESCRIPTION - AND CAN'T REMEMBER WHAT IT'S FOR.

I counted the number of Oxycontin
capsules in one of my jars.
The red and white pills have become
street drugs,
and I worry they will be stolen.
But from my *bathroom*?
perhaps from my car . . .
Newsweek had an article that described
a woman taking house tours
in order to steal this drug from
strangers' medicine cabinets.

Why is my oncologist so quick to
prescribe a drug?
Might there not be something I'm
eating, or doing,
or not eating, or not doing,
that I could change?

I wish my doctor would address the
cause,
and not the symptom.

I throw away old prescriptions.
I had one from a year ago for Ritalin.
Why would anyone have prescribed
Ritalin for me?
I never took any.

Some days I cannot open the pills —
not because of the child proof caps,
which most do not have —
but because the tabs or ridges hurt
my hands.

I have twenty-nine different
prescriptions right now.
Sometimes the bottles tumble out of
the medicine cabinet onto the floor.
I am always relieved when none falls
in the toilet.

The days I don't take any drugs,
other than my daily dose of
Xeloda, Ambien, Arimidex, Zoloft,
Synthroid and Coumadin

I feel happy.
I tell my husband
I had a good day.

It takes one of my Tylox pain pills
over 45 minutes to begin to work.
At that point, I'm usually in agony.

I wonder what permanent harm I'm
doing to myself —
by taking these drugs and combina-
tions of drugs.
Perhaps I don't want to ask.

And then there's weekly chemo.
Not a prescription exactly,
and certainly not a pill.

I have some prescriptions I've never
filled.

I have too many prescriptions.

MAY 2002

Playing with Fire

Excerpt from collaborative book

You gave me the stones' story.

Did we see them all in a line,
black with white stripes
large to small,
the ocean night after we were
 married?

Did you know that first night
we would live on an island;
that you would give me a bracelet of
 stones,
black with white stripes?

The rocks are my black jewels,
my lucky stones,
my tiny monoliths,
my prayer beads.

When we were afraid,
there were tests;
machines, x-rays, bone scans, lasers
illuminations of my bones,
ribs, spine, skull,
nuclear vision of heart,
brain, liver, lungs,
hot spots, long-smoldering,
counted, named, numbered.

Always I folded a black stone,
 white stripe
in my clenched hand.

I think I should have been afraid
of the radiation.

Instead I lay still, counted my breaths,
imagined fish swimming in my veins.
I wore the too-heavy lead necklace,
but still my neck burned,
thickened and scarred.

Twice,
two times,
I've lain aligned
in the red eye of the laser beams.

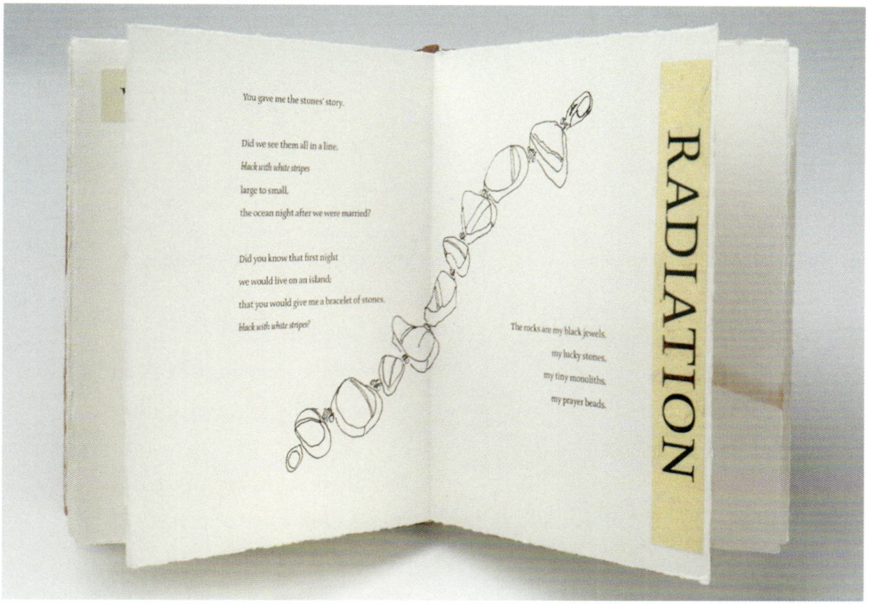

Once a day, six weeks.
Later, twice a day, eight weeks.

Eighteen times I've been injected
with nuclear medicine
to light my bones,
to photograph my pain.

Always I folded a black stone,
    white stripe
in my clenched hand.

When did you know how often
    we would hold
the black stones in our hands?

Were you afraid?

JULY 2002

Shell Bones

Emma, do you remember
Monkey Point?
We covered you with sunscreen,
    a shirt, your hat.

Your mom and dad swam
far from us, floating with the fish.
We sat on a piece of driftwood
trying to stay in the shade
that wasn't there.
We found shells,
thick,   very thick   and smooth —
not pretty like the black and white
    patterned ones
you found
later in Turtle Cove,
and made into earrings for your mom
    and me.
The Monkey Point shells
were cream or cream with pale colors.

I loved them because they were so
    heavy in my hand.
I loved them because they reminded
    me of bones.
I wanted my bones to be thick and
    strong like the shells
but I did not tell you that.

You and I decided
The shells were hundreds and
    hundreds of years old.

We piled them on a board and
made shell forts and walls.
You picked a pale yellow one
when your mom said you could only
    take one home.

But
when your mom wasn't watching,
I filled my pockets with the thickest
    shells.
They're on the windowsill now —
in the room where
You'll sleep this summer.
They remind me of you and sand and
    the turquoise
and Monkey Point

I didn't notice until today
that some of the shells have deep holes.
I didn't want them to be like my bones.

WHEN YOUR MOM SAID YOU
A PALE YELL
I LOVED THEM BECAUSE THEY REMINDED ME OF BONES
HAND.

Independence Day

July 4, 2002

I declare my independence from
    fielding complaints
about other family members.

I declare my independence from
    taking blame
when it does not belong to me.

I declare my independence from
    having to justify spending —
    yours or mine.

I declare my independence from
    listening to criticism:
of the amount of food in the pantry,
brand names vs. store brands,
organic vs. not.

I declare my independence from guilt
about long ago hurts, slights and
    mistakes,
imagined, symbolic or real.

I declare my independence from
    being responsible for others'
    immediate needs for food or drink.

I declare my independence from
    listening to monologues,
Especially when I am ill or tired or
    just need quiet.

I declare my independence
    from negativity and responding to
    sentences that begin,
"Do you know what really frustrates,
    angers, annoys or bothers me?"

I declare my independence from
    giving advice about cats or cars.

I declare my independence from
    others' moods.

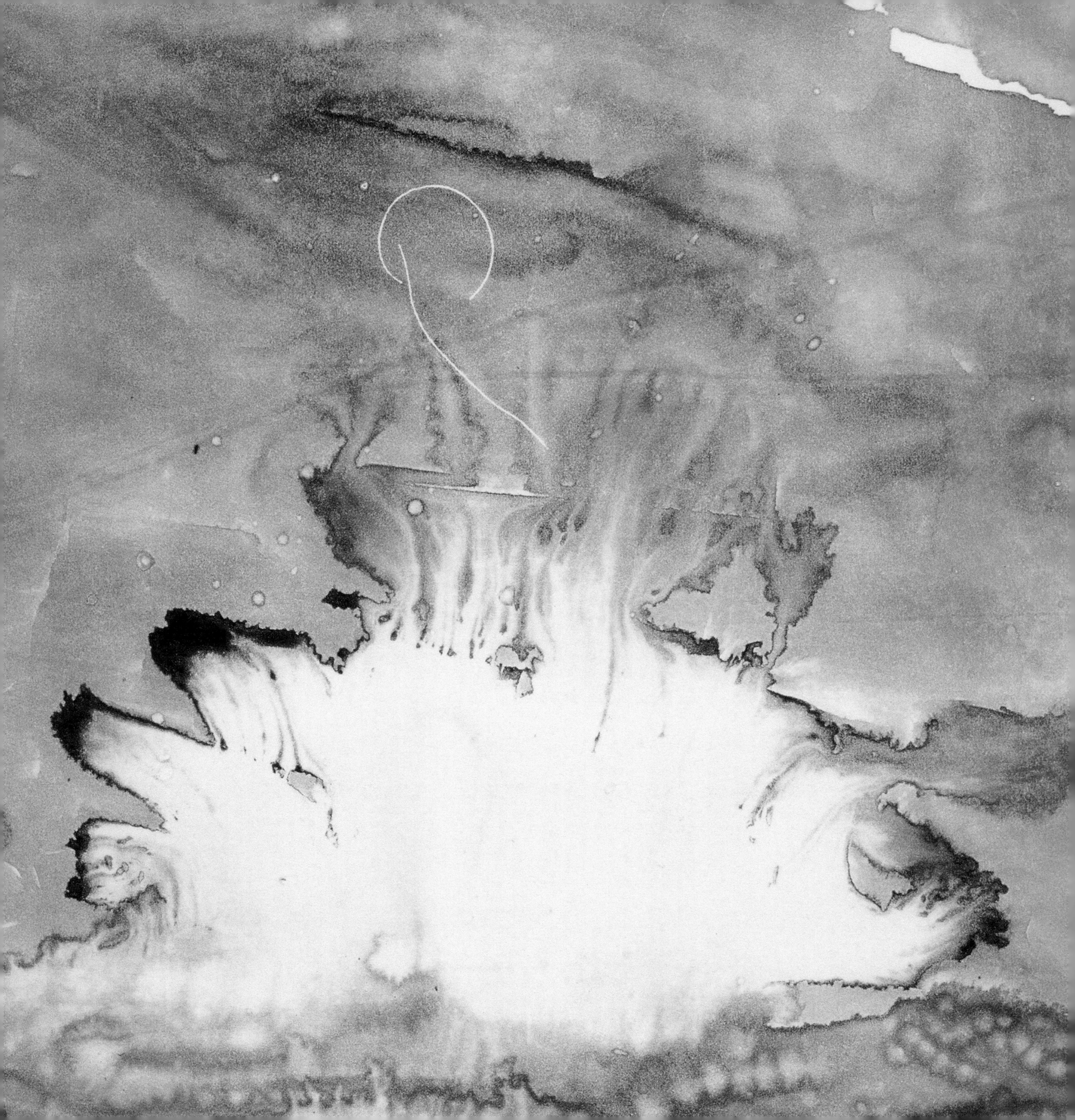

AUGUST 2002

Night

I lie awake
listening to the wind,
the waves,
waiting for the rain.

I bless the fish that swim in my veins
and dance with the moon's silver in
the cove.
I hear the heron shriek.
I watch the gray light pause.

I do not want to think of what I fear.

I take another pill.

I wander through tomorrow's
unwritten lists
and solve problems that never were.

I create music from the sounds
of your beating heart,
the rustle of the cat,
your sleeping breath.

I paint landscapes in the window
frames.

I make myself heavy under the quilt,
but I cannot push back my fears.

I do not sleep.

JANUARY 2003

Tell Me

What do you fear —
that I don't know?

What do you fear —
that I don't want to know?

What if my cancer invades
my spine,
higher, wider, greedy,
taking over more of
my bones

until I cannot stand?
cannot manage the pain?
cannot sit?

What if my cancer spreads
to my lungs?
to my brain?

What if there's nothing more
that we can do?

I am afraid
to speak my fears aloud,
to ask questions,
to hear your answers,
to know what you know,
so do not tell me.

Just turn the page
and close the book.

Do not tell me
now.

Catalogue Raisonné

1. *Treasures*
   September 1996
   Edition of 3
   Slipcase: 4 3/4" x 11 11/16" x 1 3/4"
   Single signature; dos-à-dos; accordion variation; paper covers; three books housed in slipcase
   Watercolor; paste-paper
   Handwritten in colored ink

2. *The Raven*
   November 1996
   Edition of 2
   5 1/8" x 6 1/8" x 3/8"; opens to 90 1/2"
   Accordion with paste paper boards
   Paste paper
   Handwritten in white ink

3. *Poems of Africa*
   January 1997
   5" x 6 1/8" x 1/2"; opens to 46"
   Two-sided accordion with paste paper boards
   Paste paper
   Handwritten in brown ink

4. *Support Group*
   February 1997
   8" x 9 1/2" x 1/2"
   Three signatures with paste paper wrapper
   Paste paper; collage
   Photocopied inkjet

5. *Galapagos Islands*
   February 1997
   8 1/2" x 4 1/2" x 3/4"
   Japanese stab-sewn binding with twisted cord; paper wrapper
   Color xerox photos

6. *Ecuador*
   February 1997
   8 1/2" x 4 1/2" x 1 1/4"
   Japanese stab-sewn binding with woven tape; paper wrapper
   Color xerox
   Handwritten in black ink

7. *Fog Fears*
   March 1997
   5 1/4" x 5" x 3/4"
   Accordion with paper boards; removable spine
   Collage: navigational charts, rice paper, string
   Inkjet

8. ***Just to Live*** page 18
   March 1997
   7 1/2" x 7 3/8" x 1 1/4"
   Chain and long stitch binding; eight signatures; stiff paste paper wrapper
   Mixed media collage: cloth, photo xerox, metal, medical tubing, stitching, rice paper, paste paper, postage stamps, altered envelopes, medical tests and films, watercolor
   Inkjet and handwritten in colored ink

9. ***Just to Know*** page 20
   March 1997
   7 1/2" x 7 3/8" x 1 1/4"
   Chain and long stitch binding; eight signatures; stiff paper wrapper
   Mixed media collage: metal, stitching, rice paper, paste paper, medical films
   Inkjet

10. *Test Day I*
    March 1997
    Edition of 2
    6" x 4 7/8" x 1/4"
    Single signature with metallic ribbed paper wrapper
    Suminagashi and ribbed paper
    Inkjet

All books labeled in **bold** are included in this catalog. All text by the author unless noted. All works are unique unless noted.

11. *Prayers and Dreams*
July 1997
$4^3/_4$" x $2^1/_2$" x $^1/_2$"; opens to $23^1/_2$"
Two-layer accordion with paste paper boards
Relief and intaglio prints, paste paper, rubber stamps, cut-outs

12. *First Star I*
July 1997
$5^1/_4$" x $2^3/_4$" x $^1/_2$"; opens to $14^1/_2$"
Three-layer star binding with paste paper boards and paper slipcase
Cut-outs, original stamps
Handwritten in silver ink

13. ***What Will Be My Legacy?*** page 60
July 1997
$3^1/_4$" x $5^3/_8$" x $^3/_4$"; opens to $11^1/_2$"
Three-part "Farmer's Purse" with stiff paste paper wrapper and slipcase
Collage: gold thread, cut-outs, stamps, paste paper
Rubber stamps

14. *Island Bridge*
July 1997
$3^1/_2$" x 3" x $^5/_8$"; opens to 22"
Accordion with Japanese paper over boards; Japanese paper slipcase
Hand-colored intaglio prints;
Handwritten in turquoise ink

15. *Symmetry*
July 1997
9" x $6^1/_4$" x $^1/_8$"
Single signature with pop-ups, pleated spine, paper wrapper
Hand-textured paper, slit and folded
Handwritten in black ink

16. *Haystack Views*
September 1997
$7^3/_4$" x $10^3/_4$" x $^1/_4$"
Single signature with Lokta paper wrapper and Japanese rice paper collage
Collage: paste paper, assorted found colored papers, Japanese papers

17. *Should*
September 1997
$4^5/_8$" x $4^5/_8$" x 1"; opens to 106"
Compound binding: accordion with paste paper boards, collage
Inkjet

18. *Spring and Fall*
September 1997
$9^1/_2$" x $5^3/_8$" x $^3/_8$"
Single signature with shaped pages and cut-outs, paper wrapper with reinforced spine
Color and black and white xerox transfers
Text by Gerard Manley Hopkins; inkjet

19. *Her Garden*
November 1997
$8^7/_8$" x $6^1/_4$" x $^1/_2$"; opens to 42"
Unique variation of Hedi Kyle flag structure; cover: paper boards
Color photographs, textured color papers
Text by Elizabeth Jennings; inkjet

20. *November*
November 1997
$4^1/_4$" x $4^1/_4$" x $^3/_8$"; opens to 32"
Compound binding: accordion with paper boards, paste paper slipcase
Black and white xerox
cut-outs
Text by William Dean Howells; inkjet

21. *Among Thy Trees*
December 1997
$7^3/_4$" x $6^1/_8$" x $2^1/_2$"; opens to 36"
Four-layer star binding with cut outs; paper-boards and paper slipcase
Black and white Xerox transfers, wood graining, paste paper, color photographs
Text by George Herbert; handwritten in silver ink; inkjet

22. *God's World*
March 1998
$6^1/_2$" x $9^3/_4$" x $^1/_4$"
Single signature with collograph wrapper
Collage: black and white and color xeroxes of artist's photographs, paste paper, textured colored papers, cut-outs
Text by Edna St. Vincent Millay; inkjet

23. *Books*
July 1998
4 1/4" x 3 1/4" x 1/2"; opens to 24"
Compound binding: two-sided accordion with stitched-in signatures; paste paper boards
Paste paper, colored papers
Handwritten in silver ink

24. *Haystack Dreams*
July 1998
8 1/2" x 5" x 1/8"
Single signature with staggered pages, Lokta paper wrapper
Cut outs, paste paper, colored papers
Handwritten in black ink

25. ***Living*** page 24
July 1998
Edition of 2
6 1/2" x 4 1/2" x 1/8"; opens to 34"
Accordion with paper wrapper
Hand-made paper with thread and hair inclusions
Rubber stamps

26. *Fish Prayers*
August 1998
12 1/2" x 7 3/4" x 1/4"
Stab-sewn binding with heavy paper wrapper
Hand-made paper
Inkjet

27. *Dreams and Daydreams*
August 1998
Collaborative edition of 15
7" x 5 3/8" x 7/8"; opens to 38"
Concertina with paste paper boards
Hand-made paper, collage,
Gocco printing, found materials

28. ***Voices: Five Doctors Speak*** page 26
August 1998
Edition of 12
6 1/4" x 9" x 1 1/4"; opens to 48"
Compound binding: concertina with tipped-in single pages, pockets, stitched-in signature, folded pages and a miniature book in an envelope;
Lokta paper boards
Black rubber stamp images
Inkjet

29. *First Star II*
September 1998
1 1/4" x 3 1/4" x 1/2"
Three-layer star binding with paste paper boards
Paste paper, cut-outs, rubber stamps
Inkjet

30. *Sad*
October 1998
6 1/2" x 12 1/4" x 1/4"
Japanese stab-sewn binding with stiff paper wrapper
Hand-made paper with thread and hair inclusions
Rubber stamps

31. *Shells*
October 1998
8 5/8" x 6 1/4" x 1/2"; opens to 24"
Two interlocking double-sided accordions with Lokta paper boards
Lokta papers, color photographs
Inkjet

32. *Hope*
October 1998
8" x 4 1/4" x 3/4"; opens to 48"
Accordion with cover cut-out, Japanese paper boards
Commercial metallic flecked papers, rubber stamps, feathers
Text by Emily Dickinson; rubber stamps and inkjet

33. ***Tattoo*** page 30
November 1998
Edition of 20
4 3/8" x 4 3/8" x 1"; opens to 32"
Compound binding: double-sided accordion with stitched-in signatures; printed paper boards
Colored papers, printed and paste paper, original and commercial rubber stamps, stencils
Inkjet and white colored pencil

34. ***What You Don't Want to Know*** page 34
December 1998
Open edition
9" x 5 7/8" x 1 1/4"
Altered book with sections sewn onto accordion base, paper boards
Stitched, stapled, torn, glued, cut, crumpled, marked, resequenced pages
Text by National Cancer Institute and artist; rubber stamps; handwritten in black ink

35. *Hope/Questions*
December 1998
6" x 6 1/4" x 1/4"
Single signature with folded paper cover
Collage
Found text; photocopied

36. ***Black Box*** page 35
December 1998
14 5/8" x 9 1/2" x 3"
The black box holds 10 black and white books each made with a different binding. Structures include palm leaf, flexagon, accordion, single signature, double signature, boards and paper wrappers.
Black and white photo-xerox; textured papers, collage, shadow painting
Inkjet or handwritten in ink

37. ***Test Day II*** page 38
February 1999
Edition of 11
7 1/2" x 5 1/2" x 1/4"; opens to 44"
Accordion with boards
Shadow painting
Gocco printed

38. *Harbour Island*
February 1999
13 1/2" x 6 1/2" x 1"
Flag book with paper boards
Color photographs, paste paper

39. ***Sisters*** page 40
March 1999
7" x 5 1/4" x 1/2"; opens to 32"
Flag book with paste paper boards
Black and white photo-xerox, paste paper, metallic spray painting on inkjet cover text
Gee Smith, Elise Froeberg, Laurel Smith,
Text by Martha Hall, Danielle Hall, Gabrielle Hall; handwritten in silver ink

40. *Cove Colors*
April 1999
3 5/8" x 3" x 3/4"; opens to 74"
Compound binding: accordion with stitched-in signatures; boards with paper wrapper
Photo fragments, Japanese papers
Handwritten in silver ink

41. ***Dark Room Days*** page 42
April 1999
3 1/4" x 2 3/4" x 1/2"; opens to 88"
Accordion with boards and paper wrapper
Photo fragments
Handwritten in white ink

42. *Mornings I*
May 1999
1 1/4" x 7 3/4" x 3/8"; opens to 12"
Palm leaf with Japanese paper boards linen thread with shell closing
Photographs
Handwritten in black ink

43. *Mornings II*
May 1999
1 1/4" x 7 3/4" x 3/8"; opens to 12"
Palm leaf with Japanese paper boards linen thread with shell closing
Photographs

44. *Indigo Elements*
July 1999
5 3/4" x 8 1/2" x 1/2"
Single signature with paper wrapper
Hand-made paper with embedded natural objects: moss, sticks, grasses, seaweed; burned pages; completed book dipped in natural indigo dye bath

45. *Chinese Fish Market*
July 1999
$15\frac{1}{2}$" x $15\frac{1}{2}$" x $15\frac{1}{2}$"
Wooden framework
Hand-made paper with embedded metal, nets, fibers, photographs; rubber stamps; embossing; cut-outs; metallic inks

46. *Paper Pieces*
July 1999
$6\frac{1}{2}$" x $9\frac{1}{2}$" x $\frac{1}{4}$"
Wet bound book (spine fused as wet papers couched in layers to form text block)
Hand-made paper; collage

47. *Fish*
September 1999
Open edition
3" x $5\frac{1}{2}$" x $\frac{1}{2}$"; opens to 10"
Unique structure with pages 'locked' together without stitching or paste; marbled Japanese paper envelope
Various papers, cut, folded, hole-punched
Handwritten in colored ink

48. *Sea Secrets*
October 1999
1" x 1" x $\frac{7}{8}$"; opens to $14\frac{1}{4}$"
Accordion with sea glass covers tied with metallic thread
Metallic spray painting over text
Inkjet

49. *Island Views*
October 1999
$4\frac{1}{4}$" x $3\frac{1}{4}$" x $\frac{3}{4}$"; opens to 46"
Accordion with paper wrapper
Collage: magazine and rice paper, paste paper, and colored papers

50. *Small Gems*
November 1999
$12\frac{1}{2}$" x $7\frac{1}{2}$" x $1\frac{1}{2}$"; opens to 38"
Flag book with paste paper boards and Lokta envelopes stamped with designs
Photography, rubber stamps

51. *Danielle's Tea*
December 1999
$8\frac{3}{16}$" x $5\frac{3}{4}$" x $1\frac{3}{8}$"
Found box covered with hand-made paper containing hand-painted or Japanese paper tea bags
Japanese papers; rubber stamped lettering
Artist's tea bag labels

52. ***It's Nothing*** page 44
December 1999
9" x 6" x $\frac{3}{4}$"
Variation on concertina and flag structures with paper and vellum wrapper
Acrylic ink painting
Handwritten in pencil

53. *Stones*
December 1999
$6\frac{15}{16}$" x $5\frac{5}{16}$" x $\frac{7}{8}$"
Z-form accordion with board and Lokta paper wrapper, linen threads, and shell
Colored photographs; textured colored papers
Handwritten in black ink

54. *Poems of a Winter Beach*
February 2000
6" x 8" x $1\frac{1}{2}$"
Found corrugated cardboard box with mussel shells
Drawings
Handwritten in black ink

55. *Is This a Book?*
February 2000
$12\frac{3}{8}$" x $9\frac{1}{4}$" x 2"
Blank text block with punched holes; linen thread wrapping; tied to the found fruit pack
Aging cover with ribbons
Paste painting

56. ***Inside Out*** page 48
March 2000
19" x 15" x $\frac{7}{8}$"
Concertina with paste paper boards, paper wrapper
Charcoal and acrylic ink drawings and paintings; medical CT images; black and transparent papers
Handwritten in white colored pencil

57. ***Blue Moon*** page 50
April 2000
9 1/4" x 15" x 1/2"
Japanese stab-sewn binding; clear acrylic sheets as covers, Lokta paper wrapper with found mica disc for clasp
Layered acrylic ink paintings on sheer colored papers and clear acrylic sheets
Handwritten in pencil

58. *Tea Artist's Sketchbook*
April 2000
9 1/2" x 6" x 1 3/4"; opens to 62"
Compound binding: concertina with 21 signatures stitched into peak folds; metal grommets and ribbon for hanging
Watercolor papers painted and over-painted with a variety of teas
Handwritten in ink

59. *Tea Therapy*
April 2000
12 1/2" x 9 3/4" x 1"; opens to 49 1/2" x 39 1/2"
Single sheet cut and folded in a Z-form accordion with a paper boards slipcase made by S. Mullenberg; folds and creases reinforced with medical tape
Distressed paper (wet, crumpled, folded, refolded, heated, etc.) with tea painting by Danielle Hall on one side, pencil drawings and rubber stamp images by the artist on the reverse

59. *Blue Quilt*
May 2000
10 1/4" x 10" x 1"; opens to 61 1/2" x 59 1/2"
Nine strips of paper cut, folded and hinged in a Z-form accordion with a paper wrapper and ribbon band
Paste paper with rubber stamp patterns in traditional nine patch configuration; colored papers

60. ***One Week from Today*** page 52
June 2000
18 1/2" x 12" x 1/2"; opens to 55 1/2"
Three-part portfolio covered with hand-made Cave Paper encloses loose sheets of the artist's hand-made paper
Hand-made paper with collage, printing (collograph and photo transfer), and chine collé
Handwritten with brown colored pencils

61. *Night Skies*
June 2000
10 1/2" x 10 1/8" x 3/8"
Single signature with Lokta paper wrapper
Cut, folded, torn, tied, and collaged colored papers

62. *A Moment of Pause*
June 2000
9" x 6" x 1 1/2"; opens to 44 1/2"
Compound binding: concertina with 15 signatures stitched into peak folds; linen thread for hanging
Watercolor papers painted and over-painted with a variety of teas
Text by Danielle Hall; handwritten in brown ink

63. *A Tuesday in August at Haystack*
June 2000
11 13/16" x 9 3/4" x 3/4"; opens to 136 1/2"
Accordion of paste papers and board
Paste paper painting
Text by Danielle Hall; inkjet

64. *Borrowed Bones*
June 2000
5 1/2" x 12 1/2" x 1/2"; opens to 41"
Concertina binding with linen thread 'venetian blind' closing; ribbed paper wrapper
Hand-made paper with collage, collograph, xerox transfer, photographic transfer prints with chine collé, shaped papers

65. *Collaboration*
June 2000
slip case is 5 1/2" x 4 1/4" x 2"
Three accordion structures with paper wrappers, each in commercial envelope with button and thread enclosure; Japanese paper slip case
Rubber stamps; stitching

66. *Diagnosis*
August 2000
9 1/2″ x 11 3/4″ x 3/4″
Concertina binding with hand-made wrappers
Hand-made paper, drawing, black and white xerox

67. *Haystack Tea*
August 2000
12 3/8″ x 9 3/8″ x 1/4″
Japanese stab-sewn binding with pulp-painted paper wrapper
Hand-made paper, pulp-painting with original stencils, drawing
Handwritten in colored pencils

68. *Three Generations*
August 2000
3 pieces; each 12″ x 12″ x 2 3/8″
Three related pulp-paper paintings on handmade paper, wrapped around a stretched canvas
Hand-made paper, pulp-painting with original stencils, drawing

69. *Healing Places: Haystack*
September 2000
12 3/8″ x 9 3/8″ x 1/4″; opens to 65″
Accordion with paste paper boards
Paste paper painting

70. *Mermaid*
October 2000
Slip case is 11 1/4″ x 6 1/2″ x 1 1/2″; opens to 33 1/2″ x 42 1/2″
Large nautical chart multi-folded in blue paper-covered slipcase
Acrylic ink paintings, pencil drawings
Text by Sinéad Lohan and the artist; handwritten with ink and colored pencils

71. *Compass*
October 2000
Edition of 2
4 1/2″ x 4 1/2″ x 1/4″; opens to 17″ x 12 1/4″
Accordion with cloth over boards
Color xeroxes of found paper collages by Gabrielle Hall

72. ***The Rest of My Life*** page 54
November 2000
2 1/4″ x 4 1/2″ x 3″; opens to 64″
Two-sided accordion with stiff paste paper wrapper in clamshell box with ribbon ties
Medical bandage taping, black and white xerox, paste paper painting
Medical appointment cards; planning calendar; prescribed medications in original envelopes
Handwritten in pencil, marker, ink

73. *Stamp Collection*
November 2000
Edition of 12
3″ x 4 1/2″ x 1/2″; opens to 36″ x 11 1/2″
Z-form accordion with paper boards
Rubber stamping; collage

74. ***Jane, with Wings*** page 56
January 2001
6 1/2″ x 6 1/2″ x 1 1/4″; opens to 17″
Multi-layered folding structure with paper wrapper; lift top box covered in textured and hand painted paper; polished stone 'knob'
Hand-made paper with inclusions of thread, hair, or linen; paste papers; stitching; torn pages; origami-like folding; commercial textured and sheer papers; painting
Inkjet

75. *Fluxus*
January 2001
Open edition
5 3/8″ x 5 3/8″ x 1/2″
Accordion with Kraft paper and newspaper wrapper tied with twine
Collage and rubber stamps on cover
Handwritten in black ink

76. *Fluxus Petite*
January 2001
Open Edition
2 1/4″ x 2 1/4″ x 1/4″
Accordion with Kraft paper boards, tied with white package string
Collage and rubber stamps on cover
Handwritten in black ink

77. *My Friend Elly*
February 2001
$10\frac{3}{8}$" x 9" x $\frac{3}{4}$"
Compound binding with fold-out pages and two-sided accordion bound into a single signature with paper wrapper soft crinkled paper cover
Collage; color xerox; ink drawings
Handwritten in ink

78. *Excess*
February 2001
9" x 7" x $1\frac{1}{4}$"; opens to 24"
Altered book; accordion hinged with grommets and gold ribbon; covers are ornate gold picture frames
Cut and shaped pages; collage; bead and sequin embellishment; painting

79. *Red*
February 2001
$6\frac{1}{4}$" x $7\frac{1}{2}$" x $\frac{1}{2}$"; opens to 57"
Accordion with colored paper decorative hinges and boards
Acrylic painting
Handwritten in pencil

80. *Cinderella*
March 2001
Edition of 2
$5\frac{1}{4}$" x $5\frac{1}{4}$" x $\frac{1}{2}$"; opens to 84"
Accordion with paste paper boards
Paste paper
Inkjet

81. ***Legacy*** page 60
March 2001
Open edition
$2\frac{3}{4}$" x $1\frac{7}{8}$" x $\frac{1}{4}$"
Two signatures stitched into paper wrapper
Rubber stamping
Inkjet

82. *Bees in My Legs*
April 2001
$8\frac{1}{4}$" x $4\frac{3}{4}$" x $\frac{3}{4}$"; opens to 35"
Two-sided accordion with paste paper boards
Paste paper, rubber stamps
Handwritten in gold ink

83. *On Becoming an Artist*
May 2001
$18\frac{1}{4}$" x 13" x $\frac{1}{4}$"; opens to 39"
Set of six single wax-coated hand-made paper pages in a tri-fold portfolio, covered in Lokta paper and bookcloth
Hand-made paper with collage
Handwritten and hand-painted in wax

84. ***Anxiety*** page 58
May 2001
Single signature with 'atlas' foldout
Cloth and paste paper boards
Handwritten in white ink

85. ***I Make Books (1)*** page 61
May 2001
Edition of 3 (see 98)
12" x $22\frac{1}{2}$" x $\frac{1}{2}$"; opens to $34\frac{1}{2}$"
Concertina binding with boards
Paste paper on black Arches paper
Inkjet

86. *Thirty*
June 2001
6" x $5\frac{1}{2}$" x $\frac{1}{4}$"; opens to 32"
Two-sided accordion with boards
Paste paper and other patterned and colored papers; collage

87. *Search of the Angels*
July 2001
$9\frac{1}{2}$" x $5\frac{3}{4}$" x $\frac{1}{2}$"
Single-fold signatures with Moriki paper boards
Acrylic painting, drawing, chine collé, cut-outs, stamping and texturing with natural objects (feathers, sand, wasp nest fragments)

88. *Window*
August 2001
Collaborative edition of 15
$5\frac{1}{2}$" x $4\frac{1}{4}$" x $\frac{3}{8}$"; opens to 48"
Two-sided accordion with paper wrapper in handmade envelope
Gocco printed; original stamps
Inkjet

89. *Gabrielle's Brown Book*
August 2001
8" x 14 3/8" x 1";
opens to 8" x 22 1/2" x 36"
French door with left and right two-sided accordions; cover is corrugated brown paper and bookcloth; closure is a plastic and string mailing grommet; bookcloth-covered drop-spine box by S. Mullenberg
Collaged found papers such as photographs, hymnal pages, charts, magazines, newspapers, wrapping paper, coffee mug wrappers, catalogs, CD liners, paste papers, film, wood; drawings in ink and colored pencils, stencils

90. ***Ghost Friends*** page 62
August 2001
6" x 9 1/2" x 10 1/2" opens to 15"
Sixteen single signature books with paper wrappers; each book sits in a 'slot' in an expandable file format also know as a "slinky" structure; housed in a bookcloth covered clamshell box by S. Mullenberg
Acrylic painting, reverse embossing, paste paper, transparent commercial papers
Inkjet

91. *Lullaby*
October 2001
10 1/2" x 6 3/4" x 3/4"
Five single signatures in boards
Acrylic painting, feathers painted and printed, pencil, ink and colored pencil drawings
Handwritten

92. *Paper Passages*
January 2002
Edition of 3; Collaboration with Allison Brown
box: 6 3/4" x 6 1/4" x 9 1/4"; books: 5 1/2" x 7 1/2" x [varies]
Three silk-covered clamshell boxes by S. Mullenberg hold a total of seventy books; structures include single signature, star, flag, concertina, accordion, more
Drawing, painting, photography, monotype printing, black and white xerox, stitching, collage, metal and rubber stamps
Text by Allison Brown and Martha Hall; handwritten in ink, pencil, or colored pencil; inkjet

93. *Morning, Deer Isle*
March 2002
Collaboration with Danielle Hall
portfolio cover: 15" x 14" x 1/2";
book: 14" x 13" x 3/8"
Pamphlet-stitched single signature with Lokta paper wrapper, portfolio covered in paper and bookcloth
Cut-out images; varying size papers
Text by Danielle Hall; handwritten in white ink

94. ***Small Rooms*** page 70
March 2002
slip case: 8" x 7 1/2" x 1 1/2";
opens to 7 1/4" x 26 1/4"
Two accordions, with shared central stitching, boards with paste paper; modified clamshell box by S. Mullenberg is covered with bookcloth and lined with paste paper
Paste paper; cut-outs; and clear acrylic windows
Inkjet

95. ***Test Results, January 2002*** page 73
April 2002
19 1/4" x 13 1/4" x 5/8"
Coptic binding with paper boards
Monotype prints
Text by artist; letterpress by David Wolfe

96. ***Prescriptions*** page 74
April 2002
Edition of 4
8 3/8" x 10 3/4" x 1"
Japanese stab-sewn binding with silk boards; modified clamshell box by S. Mullenberg is covered in silk bookcloth and lined with a black and white xerox collage
Color and black and white xerox, colored and patterned transparent papers
Inkjet

97. *Reliquary*
April 2002
10 1/4" x 5 1/2" x 1"
Coptic binding with Japanese marbled paper boards
Paste paper

98. *I Make Books (2 and 3)*
April 2002
Edition of 3 (see 85)
12" x 19" x 3/4"
Concertina binding with paste paper boards
Paste paper paintings
Inkjet

99. ***Playing with Fire*** page 78
May 2002
Collaborative edition of 15
7 1/2" x 5 3/4" x 1 3/4"
Japanese paper boards
Ink drawings, collage, medical films, pochoir, hot foil stamping
Laser print

100. ***Shell Bones*** page 80
July 2002
box: 3 3/4" x 7 3/4" x 2";
book: 2 5/8" x 3 5/8" x 1 1/4";
opens to 14"
Concertina with stitched single fold signatures in a heavyweight wrapper; box by S. Mullenberg holds the book in one compartment and a shell which inspired the text in the other, bone clasp
Torn paper, acrylic ink painting, paste paper
Handwritten in turquoise ink

101. ***Independence Day*** page 82
July 2002
10 1/4" x 5 7/8" x 1 3/4" opens to 37"
Flag book with Lokta paper, boards and drop-spine box by S. Mullenberg
Acrylic ink painting
Inkjet

102. *Amanda's Aprons*
July 2002
7 1/2" x 5 1/2" x 1/2"; opens to 54"
Accordion with cloth-covered boards (calico, buttons and ribbon)
Color photography, rubber stamps, collage

103. ***Night*** page 84
August 2002
Unique
18 1/2" x 13 1/8" x 1 5/8"
Silk boards, drop-spine box by S. Mullenberg
Monotypes, chine collé
Type by artist; letterpress by David Wolfe

104. ***Living II*** page 24
August 2002
Edition of 25
6 1/2" x 4 3/8" x 5/8"; opens to 34"
Accordion with self cover
Dieu Donné hand-made flax paper
Artist; letterpress of original rubber stamp Text by Tom Ervin, Becky Goodale, Jolanda; lettering by David Wolfe

105. ***Tell Me*** page 86
January 2003
box: 11" x 8" x 1 1/2"
book: 10 1/4" x 7 1/4" x 1"
Single signatures attached to spine with decorative long stitch; boards with handpainted paper onlay and drop-spine box covered with bookcloth; stitching and box by S. Mullenberg
Acrylic ink painting
Text by artist; letterpress by David Wolfe

106. *Rest of My Life II*
January 2003
Accordion with random handstitching by Danielle Hall; box by S. Mullenberg
Appointment cards, painted tissue paper, emboidery thread
Handwritten in brown, blue and black inks, pencil

107. *The Exquisite Tree*
February 2003
Collaborative edition of 15
3" x 5" x 3/4"; opens to 42"
Accordion with paste paper wrapper
Stencils, collage, drawing, painting
Text by all classmembers; handwritten in black ink

Photo Credits

18. *Just to Live*—page 18 Dean Powell
    page 19 Stephen Petegorsky
20. *Just to Know*—page 21 Dean Powell
24. *Living*—Ken Woisard page 24–25
30. *Tattoo*—page 31 Ed Wald
    page 30, 33 Stephen Petegorsky
34. *What You Don't Want to Know*
    page 34 Jay York
35. *Black Box*—page 35 Ed Wald
    page 36 Stephen Petegorsky
    page 37 Jay York
38. *Test Day II*—page 39 Jay York
40. *Sisters*—page 40 Jay York
    page 41 Stephen Petegorsky
42. *Dark Room Days*—page 42 Jay York
    page 43 Stephen Petegorsky
48. *Inside Out*—page 48 Ed Wald
    page 49 Jay York
50. *Blue Moon*—page 50 Ed Wald
    page 51 Stephen Petegorsky
52. *One Week from Today*—
    page 52 Luc Demers
    page 53 Stephen Petegorsky
54. *The Rest of My Life*—
    page 54 Luc Demers
    page 55 Stephen Petegorsky
56. *Jane, with Wings*—page 56 Jay York
    page 57 Stephen Petegorsky
58. *Anxiety*—page 58–59 Luc Demers
60. *Legacy*—page 60 Jay York
61. *I Make Books*—page 61 Dean Powell
62. *Ghost Friends*—page 62 Jay York
    page 64, 67 Stephen Petegorsky
70. *Small Rooms*—page 70 Dean Powell
    page 71 Stephen Petegorsky
73. *Test Results*—page 73 Dean Powell
74. *Prescriptions*—page 75 Dean Powell
    page 76 Stephen Petegorsky
78. *Playing with Fire*—page 78–79
    Dean Powell
80. *Shell Bones*—page 80–81
    Stephen Petegorsky
82. *Independence Day*—page 82 Jay York
84. *Night*—page 84 Stephen Petegorsky
    page 85 Jay York
86. *Tell Me*—page 87 Stephen Petegorsky

Biographica

1949 — born in June to Dwight and Gee Smith; the first of five children

1971 — received Bachelor of Arts (BA) from Smith College; majored in English

Married Alan Hall, Harvard '70

Taught 8th grade English and art through 1975 in South Portland, Maine

1972 — learned to weave and bought first loom

Earned Art Education certification

1973 — began teaching weaving; continued taking studio art courses and attending national workshops, a lifelong activity

1974 — awarded Masters of Science in Education (MSEd) from University of Southern Maine

1975 — traveled to Finland and Sweden in summer to study weaving

Taught 9th grade English and developed remedial reading program

1976 — gave birth to daughter Gabrielle

Became Director of Adult Education, Yarmouth, Maine (part-time)

1977 — taught Finnish weaving techniques in summer at Wittenburg University, Wittenburg, Ohio

1978 — gave birth to daughter Danielle

1979 — established retail store selling yarn, books, spinning and weaving supplies (Martha Hall, Inc.)

1983 — expanded Martha Hall, Inc. to national mail-order catalog business

1985 — began taking business classes (economics, calculus etc.) at University of Southern Maine

1987 — entered Masters of Business Administration (MBA) program at the Tuck School, Dartmouth College

Sold retail and mail order business

1989 — found lump in left breast; had a lumpectomy and a month later, a mastectomy

Diagnosed as Stage I Breast Cancer with no lymph node involvement

Awarded MBA with Honors, Tuck School of Business Administration, Dartmouth College

Began six month regimen of chemotherapy (CMF)

Commuted weekly by plane from Maine to New York City for job in marketing at American Express

1993 — experienced severe pain in shoulder; misdiagnosed / undiagnosed for 6 months

Diagnosed with recurrence of breast cancer; now in lymph nodes in neck; Stage IV Breast Cancer

Began high dose chemo (CAF); hospitalized at Maine Medical Center for nearly three months

Underwent autologous bone marrow transplant at Dartmouth Hitchcock Hospital

1994 — received radiation in left hip and left side of neck

Employed by L.L. Bean, Freeport, Maine, to develop marketing strategy

1995 — attended first workshop at Haystack Mountain School of Crafts, Deer Isle, Maine — "Paper Arts"

1996 — attended MECA workshop "Transformations" for women with cancer, a life-changing class

Took first book arts workshop, "Verse and Verso" with Rebecca Goodale and Dennis Gilbert at Haystack

Created first artist's book, "The Raven"

1997 — completed semester-long course, "Illuminated Autobiography" at the University of Southern Maine; explored breast cancer as a theme

Took "Pop-up Books" workshop, taught by Bonnie Stahlecker, at Haystack; met Alice Simpson and Anne McTaggart, the first of many long term friendships with book artists

Enrolled in Maine College of Art course, "The Art of the Handmade Book"

Began serving on board of Cancer Community Center, South Portland, Maine

1998 — included in exhibit "Art for the Cure"; first juried show acceptance

Found lump in the right side of my neck; biopsy confirmed cancer

Had radiation therapy – scheduled, after I showed my artist's books to my radiation oncologist, to accommodate Haystack workshop on book arts and papermaking taught by Nance O'Banion and Chris Rolik

Moved to Orr's Island home overlooking the ocean

1999 — accepted in BFA program at Maine College of Art (MECA)

Experienced persistent pain in ribs; informed my two oncologists; tests showed nothing

Took Robbin Ami Silverberg's papermaking and book arts workshop at Haystack and made first non-traditional books ("Chinese Fish Market")

Completed MECA Intensive Program for transfer students

Participated in book arts group show, "Island Friends," at the Portland Public Library, Portland, Maine

Diagnosed with metastatic breast cancer in ribs, hips, spine, skull, liver after CT and bone scans

Began treatment with chemotherapies for cancer as a chronic disease

Gave my book "Living with Cancer" to the Cancer Community Center, in honor of Jane Staley, founder

Began medical leave from L.L. Bean

2000 — started documenting work by creating an inventory database, a price list, a chronology, and having work photographed and videotaped

Ruth Rogers purchased "Black Box","Tattoo" and "Voices" for the Margaret Clapp Library, Wellesley College

Completed foundation work for Bachelor of Fine Arts (BFA) at MECA; officially a junior

Decided to make art versus continuing studies at MECA for BFA

Invited by curator Alice Simpson to show breast cancer artist's books at the Donnell Library, NYC

Made first private sale ("Voices"; to Dr. Ruben, NYC)

The Mortimer Rare Book Room at Smith College hosted solo show and artist's talk

Received invitation from The Koop Institute, Dartmouth Hitchcock Hospital, to speak to medical professionals

2001 — began to make books in multiples (e.g. "Voices" in an edition of 12; "Tattoo" in an edition of 20)

The Maine Women's Writers' Collection at the University of New England acquired a core collection of my artist's books for student use in the "Medicine and Humanities" curriculum

Took a class from Tim Ely in Easthampton, MA and began painting directly on pages

"Tattoo" included in Shereen LaPlantz book *The Art and Craft of Books*, published by Lark

Began a seven month long collaboration with fellow artist Allison Brown ("Paper Passages")

2002 — attended the annual Paper and Book Intensive (PBI)

Made first books incorporating monoprints and letterpress text; ("Test Results January 2002" and "Night"); hired D. Wolfe to print text

Had solo show at Center for the Book Arts in NYC as "artist of the month"

Accepted at first thematic shows (themes of human rights: "Tattoo" and toys and games: "Fish")

Completed first commissioned artist's book (for the University of New England)

University of New England completed editing of video "I Make Books"

PERMANENT COLLECTIONS

National Museum of Women in the Arts, Washington, DC

Bates College, Lewiston, ME

Bowdoin College, Brunswick, ME

Dartmouth College, Hanover, NH

Smith College, Northampton, MA

Wellesley College, Wellesley, MA

Williams College, Williamstown, MA

Harvard University, Cambridge, MA

University of California at Santa Barbara

University of New England, Portland, ME

University of Vermont, Burlington, VT

Yale University, New Haven CT

The Cancer Community Center, So. Portland, ME

SOLO SHOWS

"Unfolding: Life with Breast Cancer"; Artist of the Month; invitational exhibit; The Center for the Book Arts, NYC; Sept. 2002

"Borrowed Bones", Ladd Library, Bates College, February 2001

"Inside Out", Margaret Clapp Library, Wellesley College, October – November 2000

"Inside Out", Neilson Library, Smith College, October 2000

"Self Examination – Healing through Creativity", featured artist for invitational show at Donnell Library, NYC; September 2000

AWARDS

Cash merit award for "Tea Artist's Sketchbook"; Art of the Book Juried Competition of the Christel Dehaaan Fine Arts Gallery, University of Indianapolis, March – April 2002.

Special Commendation for Content for "Voices"; Book Explorations 2002; The Quest for Meaning 5th annual juried group show sponsored by The New Art Forum, Kingston, MA; April 2002.

"Outstanding Alumnus/a" award by Tuck School of Business Administration, May 2001 (first and youngest female to receive award); Boston, MA

Judges' Commendation for Excellence in Structure, Imagery and Content; "Tattoo"; Book Explorations, sponsored by the New Art Forum, Kingston, MA. Juror Anne Anninger, former curator of graphic arts at Harvard University's Houghton Library; April 2001

Tuck Scholar, Amos Tuck School of Business, Dartmouth College; 1989

The John and Sabra Hamilton Prize in Administration for the outstanding student in Strategy and Organizational Design, Amos Tuck School of Business, 1989

Elizabeth Babcock poetry prize, Smith College, 1970

BOOK ARTS LECTURES

"Elements of An Artist's Book" – Baxter Society, Portland, ME; February 2003

"Art and the Patient — Communication" – video of interview by Jennifer Tuttle, Faculty Director, Maine Women's Writers Collection, University of New England, Summer 2002

"Once in a Blue Moon", Cancer Community Center, So. Portland, ME, annual meeting keynote address; June 2001

"Artist's Books", New Hampshire Public Radio, Front Porch program; April 11, 2001

"Borrowed Bones", Bates College, March 20, 2001

"Inside Out – Artists' Books and Healing", Dartmouth Hitchcock Hospital, sponsored by the Koop Institute; November 20, 2000

"Inside Out – Creativity and Healing", Wellesley College, October 27, 2000

"Inside Out – Creativity, Artists' Books, and Healing", Smith College, October 17, 2000

Maine Public Broadcasting Network interview; October 12; 2000

PUBLICATIONS

"Words and Images", national literary and art publication of the University of Southern Maine, Portland, ME, Spring 2003

Haystack Mountain School of Crafts 50th Anniversary publication, Winter 2003

"Words and Images", annual literary and art magazine of the University of Southern Maine, Portland, ME; Spring 2002

The Art and Craft of Books by Shereen LaPlantz; published November 2001; Lark Books, Asheville, NC

DownEast Magazine, April 2001

COLOPHON

About this Catalogue

This catalogue was created by Martha Hall in collaboration with Martin Antonetti of the Smith College Mortimer Rare Book Room in the spring of 2003. Its production was made possible by generous grants from the Hawthorne-Longfellow Library at Bowdoin College, the Margaret Clapp Library at Wellesley College, and the office of the Provost at Smith College.

Special thanks to Barbara Blumenthal, Cally Gurley, Richard Lindemann, Chris Loring, Ruth Rogers, Jae Rossman, and the entire Hall family.

The type is set in Perpetua and Syntax
Designed by Carolyn Eckert
Printed by Herlin Press

Edition of 500